BE
REVIVED

BE REVIVED

KATIE SOUZA

CHARISMA
HOUSE

Most Charisma House Book Group products are available at special quantity discounts for bulk purchase for sales promotions, premiums, fund-raising, and educational needs. For details, call us at (407) 333-0600 or visit our website at www.charismahouse.com.

BE REVIVED by Katie Souza
Published by Charisma House
Charisma Media/Charisma House Book Group
600 Rinehart Road, Lake Mary, Florida 32746

Library of Congress Cataloging-in-Publication Data:
An application to register this book for cataloging has been submitted to
the Library of Congress.
International Standard Book Number: 978-1-62999-700-1
E-book ISBN: 978-1-62999-701-8

22 23 24 25 26 — 8 7 6 5 4
Printed in the United States of America

CONTENTS

CONTENTS

CHAPTER 1
THE NEW WINESKIN

S IT POSSIBLE to live disease free and unrestricted by pain? Is vibrant, long life available to those who believe that God heals? Can you look and feel better than you have in decades, without cosmetic surgery or costly procedures?

The Bible is packed full of promises that God's people can walk in divine health and have their youth restored, even in their advanced years. Yet few are seeing the full manifestation of these truths. Instead, most are suffering some sort of pain, disease, or disorder, and many are physically and mentally worn out.

To add insult to injury, every glance in the mirror confronts us with the loss of our youthful looks. It's in those moments that we toy with ideas about cosmetic procedures in a desperate effort to restore some semblance of our glory days.

I have battled all of this. I also have fought and, thankfully, conquered many physical disorders. But certain lingering issues have refused to submit. As the producer and host of an international TV show, I face more pressure than most to look great. After all, millions are watching as I age, program by program. Many viewers compliment me, but over the years, some well-meaning people have also made hurtful comments about my weight or appearance.

It's hard to grow old in front of the masses. I was well into my forties when I started my ministry, so I was already "on my way out," as some would say. I also had to deal with the ravages of my BC (Before Christ) years of partying on the streets. Hard-core drinking, smoking, and drug abuse take a toll on a person's body and appearance. The stress of ministry didn't do my health any favors either. After a decade of grueling touring, it's no wonder I started looking haggard.

However, it was menopause in my early fifties that took my battle with aging to a whole new level. This attack on my youth put years on me practically overnight! To say that I was ticked off at the devil would be an understatement.

Is it possible to tap into the youth-restoring guarantees the Word brags about—and if so, why isn't everyone running faster, serving stronger, lasting longer, and looking better while they do those things?

That's what I set out to discover. What I learned was a game changer, to say the least. I witnessed biblical truths manifesting in my life and the lives of others that left me bowing at God's feet, overwhelmed by His goodness and downright ecstatic.

Promises of Youth Restored

The Bible makes some audacious claims concerning health, long life, and the restoration of youth. Check out these examples:

> His flesh shall be fresher than a child's: he shall return to the days of his youth.
>
> —JOB 33:25, KJV

> Run to GOD! Run from evil! Your body will glow with health, your very bones will vibrate with life!
>
> —PROVERBS 3:7–8, MSG

> Wisdom extends to you long life in one hand and wealth and promotion in the other.
>
> —PROVERBS 3:16, TPT

When I first read these scriptures, their daring assertions astounded me! It seems preposterous to believe that you can live a long life *and* have strong bones and flesh fresher than a child's. Yet the Bible says His Word is absolute truth that does not return void but accomplishes that for which it was sent (Isa. 55:11). This leaves us with the burden of believing what He says, no matter how impossible it seems. To do less is to take from Christ the just reward of His suffering. After all, we have been healed by His stripes (Isa. 53:5). And yes! That encompasses all disease, including disease associated with aging.

So what's the deal? If the Scriptures contain such incredible promises, why aren't we seeing them manifest in their fullness? Ephesians 3:10 says that "through the church the complicated, many-sided wisdom of God in all its infinite variety and innumerable aspects might now be made known." The wisdom of God *is* complicated, many-sided, and infinite in its variety. I've seen thousands of jaw-dropping miracles through the ministry He has given me. However, each miracle came about because the Holy Spirit showed me complex secrets in the Word that enabled me to work the miracles.

That is essentially what this book is about. It is the result of countless hours of harmonizing Scripture so that suffering people everywhere can tap into God's fountain of youth.

The Mountain of Aging, Death, and Disease

More than a year ago the Lord showed me a vision of a huge mountain that was blocking my access to the next level. As I looked intently at it, I became troubled by the enormity of its cliffs and elevation. When I asked Him what the mountain was called, He said, "Aging, death, and disease."

People say there are two things you can always count on: death and taxes. Both are considered inevitable. As believers we understand that death is only a transitional moment. However, aging, death, and disease are at work in our bodies every single minute until we make that glorious passage. They slowly and insidiously drain our vitality, one precious drop after another, until all that remains is a withered corpse.

That day, as I stared at the mountain before me, I wondered whether it was even possible to climb what seemed so impassable. Thankfully, Jesus said that it was, and He made it sound easy:

> Jesus answered [His disciples] and said to them, "Have faith in
> God. For assuredly, I say to you, whoever says to this moun-
> tain, 'Be removed and be cast into the sea,' and does not doubt

in his heart, but believes that those things he says will be done, he will have whatever he says."

—MARK 11:22–23, NKJV

Have you ever read this verse and pictured the impossibility of a mountain jumping into the sea at your command? I have. Yet I knew God was calling me to take this mountain not with my puny faith but with His faith. That's what happened to Zerubbabel when he returned from Babylonian captivity. Amid the most adverse conditions, God called him to rebuild the temple and assured him that his "mountain" would become a mere molehill:

> For who are you, O great mountain [of human obstacles]? Before Zerubbabel [who with Joshua had led the return of the exiles from Babylon and was undertaking the rebuilding of the temple, before him] you shall become a plain [a mere molehill]! And he shall bring forth the finishing gable stone [of the new temple] with loud shoutings of the people, crying, Grace, grace to it!
>
> —ZECHARIAH 4:7

Zerubbabel and I were both called to complete essentially the same task. He had to reconstruct the temple structure; I had to learn how to rebuild the temple of the body. Each of us faced a mountain of obstacles. Zerubbabel dealt with people problems, whereas I encountered the obstacle all humans face: battling the slow, deliberate process of death that occurs over a lifetime.

As I read Zechariah 4, I could hear God mocking the enemy: "Who are you O great mountain! My people will bring forth the finishing stone of this new temple!" It would happen exactly as Zechariah prophesied: "not by might, nor by power, but by [His] Spirit"! (Zech. 4:6, ESV).

As soon as I committed myself to the battle, in my mind's eye I saw the mountain again. This time, an eagle soared over its crests. Immediately I knew that massive formation would be thrown into the sea by a revelation of renewed youth! Psalm 103:5 says, "You've supercharged my life so that I soar again like a flying eagle in the sky!" (TPT). Isaiah 40:31 adds, "Those who wait upon GOD get fresh strength. They spread their wings and soar like eagles, they run and don't get tired, they walk and don't lag behind" (MSG).

Taking the mountain of death includes walking in renewed youthfulness and beauty. So many people today have cultivated enormous influence through social media. Some make millions, even billions, just by flaunting their looks. Sadly, followers allow themselves to be manipulated by celebrities who are beautiful and seem to have flawless looks. As Christians we know our value does not come from our outward appearance. But I believe we should look amazing—not because we want to keep up with reality TV stars, but because we have conquered the mountain of unhealthy aging, death, and disease and understand the supernatural power we possess to restore our youth.

I don't know about you, but I'm tired of thinking about how I look and feel. I want the freedom to serve God and think of others first. That's why I have fiercely pursued the truths in this book. I want to tap into His supernatural power to look and feel great. I believe you want the same.

The New Wine of Revival

Certain revelations come into the earth in specific seasons. I believe this is the time for youth to be restored. After I saw the mountain vision, the Lord gave me a word: He said He was going to create *new wineskins* for His people.

What does that mean?

A wineskin is simply a container for wine. Your body is the wineskin (or vessel) that contains your spirit and soul. Age, stress, and the traumatic state of this world can cause your body to get old fast. The Bible says that when new wine is poured into an old skin, the skin bursts, and the wine is spilled. (See Matthew 9:14–17; Mark 2:18–22; and Luke 5:33–39.)

New Wine Needs a New Skin

The Lord has made clear through many prophets around the world that He is pouring out the new wine of revival in ways we have never seen before. A violent wind of change is coming from heaven that will blow in masses of people hungry for God and His salvation. As these converts come into the body of Christ and are discipled into maturity, they will need physical, mental, and emotional healing.

The harvest will be plentiful, but the laborers who are strong and healthy enough to tend the fields are few. (See Matthew 9:37 and Luke 10:2.) The body of Christ is sick and weak! When I conduct meetings, I often ask people to raise their hands if they are suffering from some sort of disease or discomfort. Shockingly, more than 90 percent respond with a cry of "Yes!"

More than ever we are being called as a body to bring the gospel of Jesus Christ to the world. But if we are not walking in the divine health Scripture promises, we might miss this historic moment. Stewarding a kingdom move is hard work and requires huge amounts of energy and strength. I should know. I have been touring in ministry for more than a decade and have wondered many times whether I could continue, because of the sheer exhaustion I faced while doing so.

If our bodies aren't in tip-top shape, we won't be able to keep up with the move of the Spirit. We need new wineskins. Otherwise the wine of revival will burst our old skins, and the new wine of the harvest will be lost. Look at what Jesus said:

> Nor do they put new wine into old wineskins, or else the wineskins break, the wine is spilled, and the wineskins are ruined. But they put new wine into new wineskins, and both are preserved.
>
> —MATTHEW 9:17, NKJV

If you are too sick, weak, or afflicted to gather the harvest (much less steward it), revival will fail. That's why the Lord promises new wineskins for His people. We need them so we can serve well as He brings

His kingdom to earth. God is not willing to lose the precious people He gathers to Himself. Nor does He want us to suffer and miss being part of His end-time move.

I don't know about you, but I don't want to miss the action because I was too old or feeble to run the race. Fortunately, God promises that He will supernaturally strengthen His people for such a time as this. Psalm 110:1–3 says that when God makes Christ's enemies a footstool under His feet, His people will volunteer freely in the day of battle. Then the psalm adds why we will be physically strong enough to do so—because we will have the dew of our youth (v. 3, ESV)!

Youth-Restoring Testimony

You can't effectively serve the Lord if your body is beset with unhealthy aging, sickness, disease, or injury. I've witnessed countless miracles that enabled people to continue doing work for God's kingdom. Bryan is a perfect example. He served the Lord through a weekly live Christian radio show and from the pulpit in a Native American ministry. Two years before he came to one of my meetings, he had been diagnosed with partial paralysis on the right side of his larynx. The doctor told Bryan the paralysis would continue to spread because there was no known cure for his condition.

The paralysis not only affected his ability to eat and drink but also to speak on his radio broadcast and minister in his meetings. A few months before Bryan came to my event, his condition had become much worse, causing him to choke when he ate certain food. He also developed increasingly long coughing attacks, which affected his ability to breathe and speak. Then, during one of my sessions, I received a word of knowledge that someone was having a problem with his larynx, and simultaneously I saw a vision of that person holding a microphone.

Bryan raised his hand, then came up on stage so I could pray for him. Immediately his throat started coming alive. After the prayer he went to lunch and tested his progress by eating some tortilla chips. That's when he discovered that he could eat without having to drink any water to wash down his food. Even when he finally took a drink, he could feel the ice-cold water going all the way down his throat, because his larynx had been totally healed.

Later Bryan reported to us that he ate a whole peanut butter and honey sandwich without drinking any water just to check out his healing. This would have been impossible for him to do before he received his miracle. We have been in contact with Bryan since, and he said he is totally healed and is able to serve the Lord with complete freedom for the first time in years! (You can watch Bryan's miracle testimony on YouTube at the link provided in the notes.[1])

Biblical Promises of Youth

There is absolutely nothing wrong with taking steps in the natural to improve your health and appearance. Every few months I get a professional facial treatment, although I have trained myself to do most skin treatments at home to save money. Once a year I also splurge on a laser skin-tightening treatment to keep the collagen in my skin stimulated. Although I am heavily against face fillers (people start to look like aliens), I do get a little Botox injected in my forehead to combat the constant scowl I have when I put on my game face. I also get my nails and hair done regularly, and I indulge in massages whenever I can. The key is to let the Lord lead you and reveal whether these practices are becoming excessive or tending toward addiction.

There is also nothing wrong with getting medical assistance in the natural for your physical suffering and pain. Medication may help. However, the side effects can be worse than the original issue. Exercise wisdom when considering the pharmaceutical route. God created plants, herbs, and superfoods that can be used as powerful homeopathic remedies to treat and even heal all kinds of diseases. I often use natural options as part of my health and fitness routine. My husband and I also eat organically and avoid sugars, GMOs, gluten, pesticides, hormones, and steroids. These substances can wreak havoc and create toxicity and deadly disease.

Ultimately, Proverbs 4:20–22 says that God's Word brings life and health to your body. The word translated "health" in verse 22 is the Hebrew word *marpê*, which means "a medicine."[2] The Word is the most powerful medicine available, and it heals without any side effects. This is just one reason it's vital to meditate on God's Word and decree it over yourself regularly, just as you would take medication on a regular schedule each day.

I want to spend the rest of this chapter sharing a list of healing scriptures you can meditate on and decree. These scriptures are related to healing, long life, and restored youth and vitality. In the appendix you will find a more extensive list of healing scriptures that address a variety of issues. I encourage you to stir up your faith for breakthrough by praying these healing scriptures often. Remember: God's Word is true! God "is not a man, that He should lie" (Num. 23:19, NKJV). All His promises are "Yes, and...Amen" in Christ Jesus (2 Cor. 1:20, NKJV)!

God sent His Word to heal you and save you from destruction (Ps. 107:20). His Word does not return to Him void but accomplishes what He desires (Isa. 55:11). So don't just study these verses; decree them over your life daily. Proverbs 18:21 says that the power of death and life are in the tongue, "and those who love it will eat its fruit" (NKJV). By speaking these verses over yourself—your body; brain, skin, and other organs; bones; muscles; face; and hair—you will create the fruit of life in every area. This is part of how you receive your new wineskin.

Before beginning your decrees, repent of any unhealthy pacts you have made with death by thinking or saying that you don't want to live a long life. Break your agreement with those words! This is a difficult, traumatic world, but when you wish for an early departure to glory, you come into agreement with the spirit of death and give the enemy legal ground from which to attack you. Your wish also blocks the flow of the supernatural power you need to have your youth renewed.

Throughout this book you will find activations, decrees, scriptures, and commands presented in various ways to promote health, healing, and restoration—spirit, soul, and body. Use them consistently, and allow God's Word to manifest His promises in your life.

Healing Scriptures and Decrees

As you speak these verses over yourself, I urge you to personalize them by inserting your name in each verse and customizing the text to address your particular circumstances. This is a powerful way of ushering life and youth into your areas of need.

Long life

> You shall walk in all the way that the Lord your God has commanded you, that you may live, and that it may go well with you, and that you may live long in the land that you shall possess.
>
> —Deuteronomy 5:33, esv

> Children, obey your parents in the Lord, for this is right. "Honor your father and mother (this is the first commandment with a promise), that it may go well with you and that you may live long in the land."
>
> —Ephesians 6:1–3, esv

> The fear of the Lord prolongs life, but the years of the wicked will be short.
>
> —Proverbs 10:27, esv

> My son, do not forget my teaching, but let your heart keep my commandments, for length of days and years of life and peace they will add to you.
>
> —Proverbs 3:1–2, esv

> For by me your days will be multiplied, and years will be added to your life.
>
> —Proverbs 9:11, esv

> And if you will walk in my ways, keeping my statutes and my commandments, as your father David walked, then I will lengthen your days.
>
> —1 Kings 3:14, esv

He asked life of you; you gave it to him, length of days forever and ever.

—PSALM 21:4, ESV

With long life I will satisfy him, and show him My salvation.

—PSALM 91:16, NKJV

Protection and deliverance from demonic sickness and death

I shall not die, but I shall live, and recount the deeds of the LORD.

—PSALM 118:17, ESV

He who dwells in the shelter of the Most High will abide in the shadow of the Almighty. I will say to the LORD, "My refuge and my fortress, my God, in whom I trust." For he will deliver you from the snare of the fowler and from the deadly pestilence. He will cover you with his pinions, and under his wings you will find refuge; his faithfulness is a shield and buckler. You will not fear the terror of the night, nor the arrow that flies by day.

—PSALM 91:1–5, ESV

The thief comes only to steal and kill and destroy. I came that they may have life and have it abundantly.

—JOHN 10:10, ESV

Because he holds fast to me in love, I will deliver him; I will protect him, because he knows my name. When he calls to me, I will answer him; I will be with him in trouble; I will rescue him and honor him. With long life I will satisfy him and show him my salvation.

—PSALM 91:14–16, ESV

When evening came, they brought to Him many who were under the power of demons, and He drove out the spirits with a word and restored to health all who were sick.

—MATTHEW 8:16

Skin miracles and restored youth

His flesh shall be fresher than a child's: he shall return to the days of his youth.

—JOB 33:25, KJV

And behold, a leper came up to Him and, prostrating himself, worshiped Him, saying, Lord, if You are willing, You are able to cleanse me by curing me. And He reached out His hand and touched him, saying, I am willing; be cleansed by being cured. And instantly his leprosy was cured and cleansed.

—MATTHEW 8:2–3

[He exclaimed] O my love, how beautiful you are! There is no flaw in you!

—SONG OF SOLOMON 4:7

Renewed strength, energy, and vitality

He gives power to the weak, and to those who have no might He increases strength.

—ISAIAH 40:29, NKJV

I can do all things through him who strengthens me.

—PHILIPPIANS 4:13, ESV

Even the youths shall faint and be weary, and the young men shall utterly fall, but those who wait on the LORD shall renew their strength; they shall mount up with wings like eagles, they shall run and not be weary, they shall walk and not faint.

—ISAIAH 40:30–31, NKJV

Healing Commands

Speak the following commands, knowing that His divine power and Word are working on your behalf.

1. I command my soul to be healed of trauma, in Jesus' name.

2. I command all diseases, bacteria, and viruses to die, in Jesus' name.

3. I command all curses to break, in Jesus' name.

4. I command all spirits of infirmity to go, in Jesus' name.

5. I command all pain and its roots to be healed, in Jesus' name.

Now, to see if your breakthrough has occurred, test yourself by doing something you couldn't do before. When you receive your miracle, please record a two-minute selfie video and email it to me at selfies@katiesouza.com. (Be sure to hold your phone in the landscape position.)

CHAPTER 2

THE LAW AND THE SPIRIT OF DEATH

ORE THAN A year before writing this book, I had a freaky encounter. I was sick at the time, and my little dog, Luke (who was fifteen years old), had been seizing for nearly twenty-four hours straight. Because Luke was up in years, many people said it was just a matter of time before the end would come. I couldn't accept that. It's one thing to go to sleep and pass on peacefully, but I didn't want him to go like this. My heart ached as I held him in my arms and prayed over his little body.

Then in the middle of the night, as we lay in bed, I sensed an evil presence entering the room. It appeared as a dark shadow that loomed over both of us; suddenly I heard its raspy breath sound my name: "Kaaaaatie."

It was creepy, like something out of the movies. Immediately I asked the Holy Spirit who it was, and He said, "It's the spirit of death. He is on assignment to kill you both."

Upon hearing this, I had the strangest response: I rejoiced as these words bubbled up in my spirit: *"The last enemy that will be destroyed is death"* (1 Cor. 15:26, NKJV). I knew that if death was coming to kill me, I must have already kicked the enemy in the face. Over the years, I had been healed supernaturally of myriad attacks including cancer, persistent bladder and yeast infections, chronic flu, severe sinus and throat issues, extreme body pain, and much more. So when death (literally) breathed down my neck, my confidence ran high.

Unfortunately, I didn't realize how fierce the battle would be. Other spirits immediately joined the battle. One was a very large spirit that appeared to be female. (I'd never seen anything like it.) She stuck her fingers deep into my thyroid, and as she did, I felt actual physical pain in that area. My body immediately entered menopause. Within two weeks I gained eight pounds of belly fat as my metabolism (which had previously burned like a roaring furnace) was reduced to a small spark. Though I only consumed a small number of calories each day, my body now responded as though I had wolfed down three cheeseburgers, multiple orders of fries, and some milkshakes in between.

That was only the beginning of my troubles. Practically overnight my private parts became dry, itchy, and painful, and my vitality vanished. I had been a ball of energy my whole life, but now I felt like a limp, wet rag. A couple of years earlier I had been supernaturally healed of fierce night sweats. They were so bad that I would wake up in a soaking wet bed, even with two fans set on high pointing straight at me. During that time, I was forced to keep a large bag of body wipes, deodorant, body spray, and a change of clothes with me at all times. Then, while teaching at a meeting, I was supernaturally healed! I never had a night sweat again, and I thought my menopause troubles were over.

But oh no... they had only just begun.

Death's visit brought a whole new level of warfare, including those dreaded hot flashes. They were different from the sweats and felt more like nuclear bombs going off in my body. They left me feeling helpless as the heat rolled up from my waist to the top of my head, consuming me in an unholy fire. That's when I remembered friends who'd suffered the same plight, and I realized how unsympathetic I had been. Trapped in the passenger seat of my car, they would be hit with a flash, and my only response would be to tell them to roll down the window! I realize now that I should have blasted the AC and offered them something ice cold to drink. I have since repented to those poor women now that I have experienced hell's fire for myself.

There were also other issues going on with me. My skin changed overnight, becoming dry, wrinkled, saggy, and baggy. My once-glorious hair turned grayer by the day, and I developed a ball of frizz bigger than my fist. When I could be at home, I worked a multitude of conditioning concoctions into my locks and wrapped my head in plastic wrap.

Unfortunately all my efforts proved fruitless. My poor husband! He got to see me wrapped in plastic and looking raggedy. Back then we had an inside joke: he only got to see the genie in the bottle, not out of it.

Jesus Came to Destroy Satan's Works—Including Sickness

One of the reasons Jesus came to earth was to "destroy the works of the devil" (1 John 3:8, NKJV). Those works involve all kinds of insidious attacks, including disease, disorder, and the theft of your youth. There are many proofs in Scripture that Satan can cause sickness and disease. Job 2:7 describes how Satan smote Job with painful boils over his entire body. Luke 11:14 tells of Jesus casting a spirit out of a mute man, which enabled the man to speak. Luke 13:11–13 details how Jesus healed a woman bowed over at the waist for eighteen years by a spirit of infirmity. (When He loosed her from the devil's control, she stood up straight!) And what about the boy who was epileptic, deaf, and mute? When Jesus cast a demon out of his little body, He healed him of every affliction! (See Matthew 17:14–18 and Luke 9:37–42.)

Claiming the mountain of restored youth means overcoming Satan's many attempts to steal, kill, and destroy! He is out to slay your body, using his demonic army and the spirit of death itself. According to Hebrews 2:14, Satan is the strongman over death, but Jesus took power away from both of them through His cross. Now you need to partake of that victory. Until you do, Satan will use death to kill you by slowly degenerating every part of your body: every organ and every inch of you.

It's Not Aging—It's the Spirit of Death

When faced with menopause, arthritis, and other diseases and disorders, most people assume it's a normal part of aging. That is *exactly* what the enemy wants! He and his demons have concocted a perfectly timed strategy to assault your body at a certain age so you write it off as "just getting old."

Don't get me wrong, demons can attack at any time. However, we tend to *expect* age-related disorders as we get up in years. And Satan is counting on it! Adult-onset diabetes, arthritis, kidney and bladder problems, dementia, Parkinson's disease, glaucoma, lung diseases, cataracts, osteoporosis, enlarged prostate, Alzheimer's disease, macular degeneration, and cardiovascular disease are just some of the conditions we have learned to accept as part of growing older.

I do believe that the so-called ravages of time contribute to these ills. However, I also believe that Satan has tricked us into accepting them as a normal part of aging. That's how he conceals the fact that he and the spirit of death are the main culprits. Thus we treat these disorders with medications instead of casting them out!

Breaking the Law

So what enables Satan and death to attack your body and cause disorders of every kind to take over? It starts when you break the laws of God; the enemy then pounces on the opportunity to accuse you. That's why 1 Peter 5:8 says, "Be sober, be vigilant; because your adversary the devil walks about like a roaring lion, seeking whom he may devour" (NKJV).

Satan's ability to release the spirit of death begins at the legal level when you break God's laws. The apostle Paul explained:

> When we were living in the flesh (mere physical lives), the sinful passions that were awakened and aroused up by [what] the Law [makes sin] were constantly operating in our natural powers (*in our bodily organs*, in the sensitive appetites and wills of the flesh), *so that we bore fruit for death.*
>
> —ROMANS 7:5

When I read this scripture, I was astounded! Breaking the law is sin, which gives death the right to attack your bodily organs! You have seventy-eight organs, including your skin, the largest organ of all. The Bible makes it clear that Satan can sow the fruit of death in your body through your lawbreaking. Here is another proof:

> I discern in my bodily members [in the sensitive appetites and wills of the flesh] a different law (rule of action) at war against the law of my mind (my reason) and *making me a prisoner to the law of sin that dwells in my bodily organs.*
>
> —ROMANS 7:23

When you sin by breaking God's law, death can take you prisoner by dwelling in your bodily organs. Unfortunately for all of us, James 2:10 says that no one can keep the whole law. Scripture says it's impossible because when you stumble in one area, you are guilty of breaking it all! Romans 7 also says that we were sentenced to death through the law. Look at what the apostle Paul said about that:

> Once I was alive, but quite apart from and unconscious of the Law. *But when the commandment came, sin lived again and I died (was sentenced by the Law to death).* And the very legal ordinance which was designed and intended to bring life *actually proved [to mean to me] death.* For sin, seizing the opportunity and getting a hold on me [by taking its incentive] from the commandment, beguiled and entrapped and cheated me, and *using it [as a weapon], killed me."*
>
> —ROMANS 7:9–11

Satan knows we were sentenced to death because of the law. So he uses it as his weapon to kill us. The law has been his legal loophole against humankind ever since the fall in the garden. Adam and Eve were once immortal beings. Death had no hold on them. However, once they listened to the devil and ate from the tree of the knowledge of good and evil, they died—not only in their spirit man but also in their physical bodies. They didn't die instantly, but their bodies began to degenerate slowly until death took them completely.

The law is much like the tree from which they ate. It provides us with the knowledge of what is good and what is evil. Romans 7:12 says the law is holy. We need it to help us avoid sin. Paul wrote, "I would not have known sin except through the law. For I would not have known covetousness unless the law had said, 'You shall not covet'" (Rom. 7:7, NKJV).

The problem is that as we come to know the law, it incites our rebellion against it, bringing forth sin and death. Paul said, "The very legal ordinance which was designed and intended to bring life actually proved [to mean to me] death" (Rom. 7:10).

I have firsthand experience with this. When I was on the streets, I committed many crimes. I was a meth user and a "collector," meaning I went after people who owed me or someone else money. I was arrested twelve times in a single year and eventually received a twelve-and-a-half-year prison sentence. But while I was on the streets, I felt my heart being enticed to break the law. The bigger the crime and the greater the risk, the more I wanted to do it. Why? I believe my desire was awakened by the law's prohibitions, so I craved doing the very thing the law warned against.

Lawbreaking leads to death. Paul said, "The code [of the Law] kills" (2 Cor. 3:6). He then called the commandments "the dispensation of death engraved in letters on stone [the ministration of the Law]" (2 Cor. 3:7). This death is not only spiritual but also physical, as the sin of Adam and Eve shows. When they lost their immortality, their physical aging began, and they eventually perished.

Christ Overcame Death for Us

If keeping all the commandments is impossible, how can you stop the effects of death on your bodily organs? Let's systematically look at the Bible's answers to this unrelenting assault, the first and foremost being Christ Himself!

> Christ purchased our freedom [redeeming us] from the curse (doom) of the Law [and its condemnation] by [Himself] becoming a curse for us, for it is written [in the Scriptures], Cursed is everyone who hangs on a tree (is crucified).
>
> —GALATIANS 3:13

Christ redeemed you from the curse of the law by becoming a curse for you. On the cross He took your infirmities and bore your sicknesses, including the ones Satan and death brought on you through your law-breaking. (See Matthew 8:17.) At Calvary, Jesus stripped away the power of Satan and death to oppress you!

> Since therefore the children share in flesh and blood, he himself likewise partook of the same things, that through death he might destroy the one who has the power of death, that is, the devil.
>
> —HEBREWS 2:14, ESV

By dying on the cross, Jesus partook of death on your behalf and destroyed the devil's power over you. Romans 8 goes on to explain that at the moment you received Christ, you were set free from the law of sin and death because Christ fulfilled the law *for you.*

> There is therefore now no condemnation for those who are in Christ Jesus. For the law of the Spirit of life has set you free in Christ Jesus from the law of sin and death. For God has done what the law, weakened by the flesh, could not do. By sending his own Son in the likeness of sinful flesh and for sin, he condemned sin in the flesh, *in order that the righteous requirement of the law might be fulfilled in us.*
>
> —ROMANS 8:1–4, ESV

Jesus did not come to abolish the law (Matt. 5:17–18). Rather He fulfilled the law's righteous requirements in you through His cross! His unparalleled work did what you could never do. Therefore you are no longer under the law of sin and death. Nor do you have to endure the devil's continual condemnation over your failures in keeping the law. You have been delivered from the spirit of death and are now living under the law of the Spirit of life!

The Spirit of Life

Now that Jesus has fulfilled in you all the righteous requirements of the law, you are no longer bound and controlled by it. Instead you are led by the Holy Spirit, who is the Spirit of life.

> But now we are discharged from the Law and have terminated all intercourse with it, having died to what once restrained and held us captive. So now we serve not under [obedience to] the old code of written regulations, but [under obedience to the promptings] of the Spirit in newness [of life].
>
> —ROMANS 7:6

This scripture can cause intense reactions when it's read to a law-based church. When you tell people that they don't have to serve under obedience to the old code of written regulations, they flip out. They think you are saying they don't have to obey God's law and are free to act any way they want. But that is the furthest thing from the truth.

According to Paul, you are no longer under the law but under obedience to the Spirit's promptings in newness of life. Think about it! Because the Holy Spirit lives in you, He can correct you the moment you get off track. How many times have you been telling somebody off, and in midsentence you felt the conviction of the Holy Spirit to shut up? Has He ever stopped you at the checkout and said, "That's enough spending for today"?

The written laws in the Old Testament don't tell you which school to send your children to or whom to marry. The old written code cannot lead you step by step through the daily decisions you need to make in this modern world. Neither can it correct you second by second every time you step out of God's will. Only the Spirit of life can do that!

Romans 2:15 says God's laws are now written in your heart. It is the Holy Spirit who prompts you to follow them. Therefore, you are under the "Spirit in newness [of life]" and not under the law (Rom. 7:6). You see, life is the exact opposite of death. The Holy Spirit who lives within you brings this newness of life, constantly correcting your thoughts,

21

decisions, emotions, behaviors, and motivations. When you do something displeasing to God, He nudges you and reminds you that you are off course. *Then it's your responsibility to make changes as the Spirit leads.* When you do, the Spirit who brings life will counteract the effects of death that came from trying to keep the old written code in your own strength.

Scripture confirms this truth:

> For those who live according to the flesh set their minds on the things of the flesh, but those who live according to the Spirit set their minds on the things of the Spirit. For to set the mind on the flesh is death, but to set the mind on the Spirit is life and peace.
>
> —ROMANS 8:5–6, ESV

Testimony of the Power of Life Over Death

I've seen astounding miracles happen when the Spirit of life crushes death. I was in Albany, Oregon, speaking at a key prophetic conference. As soon as I entered the room, I knew God's power was present to heal. I quickly moved the people into worship and the working of miracles. When I asked whether anyone was between 80 and 100 percent healed, people immediately ran toward the front.

One of them was a woman named Terry. As she approached the platform, I saw tears in her eyes. While grinning broadly, she yelled, "One hundred percent!"

I quickly brought her up to testify. She told me she had been diagnosed with a "dead bone" in her arm. When I asked her to clarify, she explained that the ball end of the upper arm bone was completely dead, as verified by multiple X-rays and MRIs. When I asked if she'd suffered any complications from the condition, she confirmed that she had. Even though the bone was dead, she had experienced level-ten pain every day. (She called it excruciating.) Although she could bend her elbow, she could not raise her arm at all. When I asked her to test the miracle by raising her arm, she thrust both arms in the air in a victory stance.

The crowd screamed!

During the interview, Terry revealed that she had surgery scheduled just weeks away. I said, "Not anymore, baby!"

Again the crowd lost it as she flung her arms up and down with a huge smile on her face and absolutely no pain. Death had been defeated by the Spirit of life! (You can see Terry's miracle at the link provided in the notes.[1])

Once, while doing a live broadcast to the entire world on our network, Faith TV, I received a word of knowledge. Right in the middle of preaching, I heard the word *necrosis*. Necrosis is "a form of cell injury which results in the premature death of cells in living tissue."[2] Immediately I knew that someone was dealing with the spirit of death. So I stopped preaching and decreed soul healing to that person. Next I commanded those cells to die and new, living ones to take their place. Then I continued preaching.

When I was done, I headed to the green room. A woman quickly caught up to me and pulled me aside, saying, "Sister Katie, that was me! I'm the one with the necrotic flesh!"

When I asked her what happened, she said she had been diagnosed months prior. Her upper thighs were covered with sores where her flesh had been eaten away. Doctors prescribed medications for her, but none helped. Then she added, "But when you said that word of knowledge, I felt the power of God come on me. So I immediately ran back to the bathroom to check, and all the sores were gone!"

She was totally healed!

Don't forget that the skin is the body's largest organ. The Spirit of life had overcome the spirit of death that was working in the woman's organs, through the name of Jesus Christ.

Don't Get Out of Balance

As believers we want to please the Lord. Part of that is walking in obedience. However, it is easy to cross the line between Spirit-led works and the keeping of the law through religious rituals.

I remember a season when I was in all-out war. I put my faith in seeing God's healing promises manifested—and boy, did I need it! I was sick, downtrodden, and horribly oppressed by the devil. So I went to work doing what I thought would get me the breakthrough. Every day, I spent a certain amount of time in worship, followed by a set time of Bible reading (which included reading a list of Bible decrees). I fasted from food and TV regularly and did other things I thought would get the Lord to move on my behalf.

To be clear, there is nothing wrong with any of these activities. In fact they are essential to a healthy relationship with Jesus. However, the spirit in which they are done determines the amount of power released. At the time, I didn't realize what my thinking was, but I believed that reading, fasting, and decreeing for a certain number of hours would make God love me more. Then He would "have to" fulfill His promises to me.

Needless to say, it didn't work. In fact my illness increased, and I felt worse than ever! I could not figure out what was going on, because as far as I could tell, I was doing everything right. Then one day, in total desperation, I cried out to the Lord. He gave me this stunning verse:

> All who depend on the Law [who are seeking to be justified by obedience to the Law of rituals] are under a curse and doomed to disappointment and destruction, for it is written in the Scriptures, Cursed (accursed, devoted to destruction, doomed to eternal punishment) be everyone who does not continue to abide (live and remain) by all the precepts and commands written in the Book of the Law and to practice them.
>
> —GALATIANS 3:10

I was in total shock. This verse says that when you try to be holy and in right standing with God through religious rituals, you are put under a curse. No wonder things were getting worse for me!

I believe countless Christians have lost their balance when it comes to keeping the law. Instead of running to the One who fulfilled the law's righteous requirements in them, they are trying to do the work themselves through excessive religious rituals. Without realizing it, they have put themselves under the curse of the law and are "doomed to disappointment and destruction."

Look at what the Book of Romans says about this:

> For no person will be justified (made righteous, acquitted, and judged acceptable) in His sight by observing the works prescribed by the Law.... [All] are justified and made upright and in right standing with God, freely and gratuitously by His grace (His unmerited favor and mercy), through the redemption which is [provided] in Christ Jesus.
> —ROMANS 3:20, 24

You are justified, acquitted, and made right with God through Jesus, not by keeping the law. Attempting to obey the law in your own strength is very different from doing good works. Worship, reading the Word, and fasting are vital to building intimacy with the Lord. In those private times with Jesus, you hear His heart, learn from Him, and are led by His voice toward your breakthrough. But when you turn your special time with Him into works of the flesh, you get out of balance.

Ask the Holy Spirit to show you the motives behind your spiritual disciplines. Are you doing them to get closer to Jesus and hear His voice or to win brownie points with God? Remember, you must stay in balance, or you will put yourself back under the law of sin and death instead of living under the Spirit of the newness of life.

Activation: Freedom in the Spirit of Life

1. I repent for any attempts to "be justified by obedience to the Law" (Gal. 3:10).

2. I ask the Holy Spirit to help me achieve balance in my pursuit of God.

3. I repent for any occasions when I have sinned and broken the law. I also ask the Holy Spirit to reveal any "lapses" or "hidden [and unconscious] faults" of which I am unaware (Ps. 19:12) so I can correct those behaviors and revoke Satan's right to accuse me.

4. I decree that I am no longer under the curse of the law because Jesus became a curse for me on the cross.

5. I decree that on the cross Jesus fulfilled the righteous requirements of the law in me.

6. I decree that by dying on the cross, Jesus made of no effect the one who had the power of death—Satan (Heb. 2:14).

Healing Commands

Speak the following commands, knowing that His divine power and Word are working on your behalf.

1. I command my soul to be healed of trauma, in Jesus' name.

2. I command all curses to break, in Jesus' name.

3. I bind death's actions on my bodily organs, in Jesus' name. (List your organs and bind death off each one.)

4. I command all spirits of infirmity to go, in Jesus' name.

5. I command all diseases, bacteria, and viruses to die, in Jesus' name.

6. I command all pain and its roots to be healed, in Jesus' name.

7. I ask for the Spirit of life to be released into every organ in my body and every part of my frame, from head to toe (including bones, blood, tissues, etc.), in Jesus' name.

Now, to see if your breakthrough has occurred, test yourself by doing something you couldn't do before. When you receive your miracle, please record a two-minute selfie video and email it to me at selfies@katiesouza. com. (Be sure to hold your phone in the landscape position.)

CHAPTER 3
GRACE DEFEATS THE SPIRIT OF DEATH

F OR MANY YEARS the theological concept of grace seemed so impenetrable in its mystery that I couldn't fathom it. Unfortunately, during that time, there was also a fierce battle concerning the topic. Grace teachers were coming out of the woodwork, including those who leaned far into a hyper-grace message. Old-school peeps reacted violently. It was a battle that I wanted to steer clear of. So I stayed in my lane, teaching soul healing and seeing massive fruit.

When the battle waned and the dust settled, I decided to study grace so I could find the balance between two messages that had extremes on both sides. It wasn't easy. Grace is a deep subject, and it could take until Jesus comes to totally comprehend it. But during my time of study, the Holy Spirit showed me powerful insights. I soon realized how much we need grace and its magnificent power to transform our lives.

Grace Appropriates the Power of the Cross

In this book I will not cover the vastness of this subject, but I will show how grace enables us to defeat the spirit of death so we can have our youth restored.

At Calvary, Jesus fulfilled the righteous requirements of the law on our behalf and stripped away Satan's power over death. Grace enables you to partake of these victories. Ephesians 2:8–9 says, "For by grace you have been saved through faith, and that not of yourselves; it is the gift of God, not of works, lest anyone should boast" (NKJV). You are saved *by* grace *through* faith.

When the Bible talks about salvation, receiving Jesus as Lord and Savior is part of it but not all of it. The word translated "salvation" is the Greek word *sōzō*, which means "to save, i.e. deliver or protect... heal, preserve... (make) whole."[1] This indicates that your salvation includes healing for your body, deliverance and protection from the enemy, preservation from death's decay, and the ability to be made whole and healthy.

It is beyond our comprehension to know all that Jesus won through the shedding of His blood. But one thing is for sure: the only way you can appropriate it all is by grace through faith. *Grace is the power that transmits, imparts, conveys, and diffuses these blessings into every part of your existence. Without it you could never partake of the death-destroying power of the cross.*

When Grace Abounds

It's impossible to keep the whole law, so God's grace supersedes it for you. The apostle Paul explained how:

> Then Law came in, [only] to expand and increase the trespass [making it more apparent and exciting opposition]. But where sin increased and abounded, grace (God's unmerited favor) has surpassed it and increased the more and superabounded.
>
> —ROMANS 5:20

Grace trumps the law. To trump something means to gain an advantage over it. When the sin of your lawbreaking increases and abounds, grace surpasses it and superabounds! When I read that verse, hope swells in my heart because I *need* grace. So do you. How many times a day do you unintentionally (or even deliberately) break God's law? Have you fallen into alcohol abuse or adultery? Do you get irritated and short with your spouse? It's all sin, and the enemy loves when you do it. He unmercifully uses every one of your offenses to accuse you so he can put death to work in your bodily organs. However, when your sin abounds, God's free, unmerited, and undeserved grace supersedes it!

What does that mean on a practical level? Suppose you slip up and sin during the course of your day. You can bet in that moment that the devil is joyfully rubbing his hands together, eager to bring the spirit of death on you. But when you know you have access to God's free, unearned grace, you can immediately shut Satan down! Just repent of your sin and say, "Where my sin increased and abounded, God's grace has surpassed it, increased the more, and even superabounded!"

I remember a time when I screwed up and the devil wasted no time in attacking me because of it. Immediately I felt pain in my body from his assault, so I repented of my sin, then began reading the truth of grace over my life. Within fifteen minutes the pain totally lifted!

The devil hates grace because it triumphs over the law. Let's look at more proof: "For sin shall not [any longer] exert dominion over you, since now you are not under Law [as slaves], but under grace [as subjects of God's favor and mercy]" (Rom. 6:14).

A slave is "a person who is the legal property of another and is forced to obey them."[2] The Bible says the law is holy, but because of the weakness of our flesh, we could not keep it. That is why Jesus came to keep it for us. The enemy uses the weakness of our flesh and the inability for us to keep the whole law as his legal right to assault us with the spirit of death. But Christ purchased your freedom; thus, you are no longer a slave but a subject of God's free grace! This truth is the death knell to Satan.

Grace and Righteousness

Second Corinthians 5:21 says that Christ (who knew no sin) became sin for you in order that you could be made the righteousness of God in Him. That's important because righteous people aren't considered by God as lawbreakers. Even though you still sin, Christ's sacrifice has declared you righteous in God's sight. Wow! That's grace—the power that imputes His righteousness to you.

> We are justified (acquitted, declared righteous, and given a right standing with God) through faith.... Through Him also we have [our] access (entrance, introduction) by faith into this

grace (state of God's favor) in which we [firmly and safely]
stand.

—ROMANS 5:1–2

Notice that you have not only been justified with God but also
acquitted! When the enemy accuses you of breaking the law, you can
come right back at him and say, "Yes, but I have repented, and because
of Christ and His grace, I am guiltless!"

This shuts down the enemy's attempts to work death in your bodily
organs. Paul explained how Jesus flipped the equation to your benefit:

> For if because of one man's trespass (lapse, offense) death
> reigned through that one, much more surely will those who
> receive [God's] overflowing grace (unmerited favor) and the
> free gift of righteousness [putting them into right standing
> with Himself] reign as kings in life through the one Man
> Jesus Christ (the Messiah, the Anointed One).
>
> —ROMANS 5:17

From the moment Adam broke the law, death ruled and controlled
every human being. That is, until the second Adam came. The Bible
calls Him "a life-giving Spirit"! (1 Cor. 15:45). Now, because of His grace,
we can reign as kings in life. Thus we are no longer bound under the
spirit of death!

Grace Imparts Life and Strength to the Body

Grace is a power that releases *all* God's blessings into your life.

> For out of His fullness (abundance) we have all received [all
> had a share and we were all supplied with] one grace after
> another and spiritual blessing upon spiritual blessing and even
> favor upon favor and gift [heaped] upon gift. For while the
> Law was given through Moses, grace (unearned, undeserved
> favor and spiritual blessing) and truth came through Jesus
> Christ.
>
> —JOHN 1:16–17

Through the power of grace, you can be heaped up with one blessing after another—including the power to heal and strengthen your physical body and restore it from the effects of death. The apostle Paul experienced this firsthand. He was a hardworking man who traveled extensively, preaching everywhere he went. He was also a tentmaker who earned his own way in life. During his ministry trips, Paul suffered a litany of physical trials, including many brushes with death. Look at this shocking list:

> {Are they servants of Christ?} I am more, with far more extensive and abundant labors, with far more imprisonments, [beaten] with countless stripes, and frequently [at the point of] death. Five times I received from [the hands of] the Jews forty [lashes all] but one; three times I have been beaten with rods; once I was stoned. Three times I have been aboard a ship wrecked at sea; a [whole] night and a day I have spent [adrift] on the deep; many times on journeys, [exposed to] perils from rivers, perils from bandits, perils from [my own] nation, perils from the Gentiles, perils in the city, perils in the desert places, perils in the sea, perils from those posing as believers [but destitute of Christian knowledge and piety]; in toil and hardship, watching often [through sleepless nights], in hunger and thirst, frequently driven to fasting by want, in cold and exposure and lack of clothing.
>
> —2 CORINTHIANS 11:23–27

How on earth did Paul survive such brutality and hardship? He must have tapped into some kind of power not only to keep on ministering but also to be totally healed after countless stripes from a whip, beatings with rods, three shipwrecks, and food and sleep deprivation. It's obvious that something supernatural was going on. But what was it?

Paul said it was grace!

> By the grace of God I am what I am, and his grace to me was not without effect. No, I worked harder than all of them—yet not I, but the grace of God that was with me.
>
> —1 CORINTHIANS 15:10, NIV

Grace enabled Paul to endure all those trials, but it is also why his body was healed and made whole after every brush with death. His stoning in Lystra is a shocking example (Acts 14:19–21). The Jews stoned Paul and dragged his body out of the city, believing he was dead. Yet when the disciples gathered around him, he stood up, perfectly healed! The next day he accompanied Barnabas to Derbe, where they preached the gospel! When I read that, I thought, "How in the world could a person in Paul's condition get up and immediately travel to another city to preach?"

The answer is grace! Grace not only defeats the law of sin and death but saturates believers with the ability to remain physically strong and resilient. Grace is a supernatural power that empowers us to work healing miracles of every kind. Stephen's ministry is proof, as the Bible shows: "Stephen, full of grace (divine blessing and favor) and power (strength and ability) worked great wonders and signs (miracles) among the people" (Acts 6:8). Stephen walked in the power of grace, which enabled him to work astounding healing miracles!

God's grace is inexhaustible. Acts 14:3 says that as Paul and Barnabas continued preaching "the Word of His grace," God granted "signs and wonders to be performed by their hands." The more grace you appropriate, the more miracle-working power and authority you possess to destroy death, unhealthy aging, sickness, and disease. Grace will even empower you to rebuild your temple, which is your body. Don't forget: the Bible says that Zerubbabel would "bring forth the finishing gable stone [of the new temple] with loud shoutings of the people, crying, Grace, grace to it!" (Zech. 4:7). The same grace will turn *your* mountain of death into a mere molehill.

Abraham, Sarah, and the Fountain of Youth

Have you ever wondered how Abraham and Sarah could possess physical youth in their old age and even conceive a child? It was through the power of grace. Let's look at it.

Sarah was so gorgeous that two different kings kidnapped her on separate occasions! (See Genesis 12:10–20 and Genesis 20:1–18.) The first was Pharaoh, the king of Egypt, who took her when she was sixty-five years old. The second was Abimelech, the king of Gerar, who took Sarah when she was ninety. If kings fought over this woman, you know she had it going on! She also gave birth to Isaac at age ninety. That means God caused her uterus, ovaries, thyroid, and other reproductive parts to operate perfectly even though she was well beyond childbearing age.

Abraham also walked in restored youth. At age one hundred he fathered Isaac, and after Sarah died, he remarried and had six more children. (See Genesis 25:1–2.) Scholars estimate that he was around 140 at the time![3]

Both Abraham and Sarah walked in youth-restoring power, but it hadn't always been so. At one point they both lived under the power of the spirit of death. Romans 4:19 says that Abraham's body was utterly impotent and "as good as dead" and Sarah's womb was barren and "deadened." By the looks of it, their physical bodies were as dead as doornails! In fact they were so far gone that when God promised to regenerate their youth and give them a son, even Abraham (the father of faith!) "fell on his face and laughed and said in his heart, Shall a child be born to a man who is a hundred years old? And shall Sarah, who is ninety years old, bear a son?" (Gen. 17:17).

Abraham was shocked! So was Sarah, who "laughed to herself, saying, After I have become aged shall I have pleasure and delight, my lord (husband), being old also?" (Gen. 18:12).

Because of the condition of their aging bodies, God's promise seemed absurd to both Abraham and Sarah. Yet it came to pass.

How did that happen? Some write it off to the fact that people lived longer in those days. However, it appears from the previous verses that even Abraham and Sarah knew how impossible it was for people their age to have a baby.

So how *did* it happen?

I believe grace destroyed the power that death held on their bodies. The apostle Paul confirms this in Romans 4:19, where he says Abraham "did not weaken in faith when he considered the [utter] impotence of his own body... {or} the barrenness of Sarah's [deadened] womb." Paul explains why Abraham was so confident:

> Therefore, [inheriting] the promise is the outcome of faith and depends [entirely] on faith, in order that it might be given as an act of grace (unmerited favor), to make it stable and valid and guaranteed to all his descendants—not only to the devotees and adherents of the Law, but also to those who share the faith of Abraham, who is [thus] the father of us all. As it is written, I have made you the father of many nations. [He was appointed our father] in the sight of God in Whom he believed, Who gives life to the dead and speaks of the nonexistent things that [He has foretold and promised] as if they [already] existed.
>
> —ROMANS 4:16–17

Theologians interpret this passage to mean that we are justified and made free from the law by faith in Jesus Christ. Because you have been released from the effects of trying to keep the law in your own strength, the spirit of death can be broken off your body, and the power of life can take its place. This is how Abraham and Sarah inherited the promise of restored youth. It was by grace through faith, not because they were "devotees and adherents of the Law." In fact verse 16 says that grace *guaranteed* the promise of their bodies becoming so youthful that they could conceive a child! And this miracle was not only for them. As the passage states, it is for all "those who share the faith of Abraham," our father.

From Death to Life Through Grace

Right now you might be under the spirit of death and its work in your bodily organs. Your situation might look so bad that you think it's too late to recover. That's exactly what Abraham and Sarah thought when they laughed at God. Yet God "gives life to the dead and speaks of the nonexistent things," foretelling and promising them as though they already existed (Rom. 4:17). God wants to renew your youth "like the

35

eagle's" (Ps. 103:5). The atoning work of Christ and His grace will make it happen!

In the Book of Job, Elihu described man at a point when he had suffered horribly and was at death's door.

> He is chastened with pain upon his bed and with continual strife in his bones...so that his desire makes him loathe food, and even dainty dishes [nauseate him]. His flesh is so wasted away that it cannot be seen, and his bones that were not seen stick out. Yes, his soul draws near to corruption, and his life to the inflicters of death (the destroyers).
>
> —JOB 33:19–22

The spirit of death attempted to take man out! His flesh was so wasted that his bones stuck out! He suffered this continual pain and was so far gone that he could not eat. So what happened? God's grace regenerated that man and restored his youth!

> Then [God] is *gracious* to him and says, Deliver him from going down into the pit [of destruction]; *I have found a ransom (a price of redemption, an atonement)*! [Then the man's] flesh shall be restored; it becomes fresher and more tender than a child's; he returns to the days of his youth.
>
> —JOB 33:24–25

Wow! Instead of being wasted, his flesh was restored and fresher than a child's! He was so regenerated by the power of grace that he returned to the days of his youth. And God provided an atonement for you too! His Son paid the price of death on a cross to redeem you from your lawbreaking state. Now by grace through faith, you can appropriate all that Christ won for you—including having your flesh become fresher than a child's as you have your youth restored!

Let's be real: When was the last time you saw your face and your nakedness in the mirror and quickly shut your eyes in horror? The word translated "flesh" in Job 33:25 is *basar*, which means "skin" and "body, (fat, lean) flesh(-ed)...nakedness."[4] I believe the passage from Job speaks of grace that will empower you to have youthful skin, build and firm your lean muscle, and trim down your fatty flesh.

I firmly believe in exercising and eating right. But don't forget that grace gives you supernatural power for miracles. It enabled Paul to heal from all types of injuries, including those that brought him close to death. It also empowered Stephen to work healing miracles of every kind. This passage in Job promises to restore your skin and nakedness to the freshness of your youth—fat included—through the power of God's grace!

That's not all that's contained in Job 33. The Hebrew word translated "fresher" in verse 25 is *ruwtaphash*, which means "to recover, to revive after sterility."[5] When I saw this, I almost jumped out of my skin—no pun intended! I believe this means that even if you're already in menopause (whether male or female), you can be revived and become fertile again!

That is what happened to Abraham and Sarah. They were once impotent and dead in their bodies, but God's grace delivered them from their sterility. That is great news to those who have been unable to have children. It's also an amazing promise for people who have lost their youthful looks to menopause.

What are you facing? Is it impotency or infertility? Have you become dried up, wrinkled, and old looking? Have you gotten sick and weak with disease? Are your muscles atrophying while your body fat increases? According to the Book of Job, it doesn't matter! Even if your ovaries and uterus have been removed, your thyroid has died, your metabolism has dwindled, and your testosterone, estrogen, and progesterone levels are down to zero, it's not too late. God has found an atoning sacrifice for you in His Son. By His grace your flesh can become fresher than a child's. You can be revived from your sterility and return to the days of your youth!

Miracle Testimonies

The more you learn about grace and appropriate its power, the more healing you will experience, and the more you will move in signs, wonders, and miracles, like Stephen did. I've seen the power of grace perform countless miracles in our meetings.

I was in South Africa shooting eighteen television programs when miracles broke out in the studio audience. It started when I received a word of knowledge about someone's bladder being healed. When I asked who had issues in that area, a woman raised her hand. She had participated in an obstacle-course race, fallen off a balance beam, and badly injured herself. She went to the bathroom in extreme pain and saw an alarming amount of blood in her urine. The hospital team performed an MRI and found that her urethra (the bladder's urine duct) was torn. She was treated with pain meds, antibiotics, and anti-inflammatories. The bleeding eventually stopped but only temporarily.

That day in the studio, it returned with a vengeance, and so did her pain. Just when she told her friend she needed to leave, I gave a word of knowledge. As I prayed for her, the power of grace was released into her body, and her bleeding and pain instantly stopped as her urethra was supernaturally mended. She was also healed of a bacterial infection she had developed since the accident. Later I saw her dancing fiercely and praising God as she and her friend celebrated Him and His goodness.

During the same taping, I received another word of knowledge about bone matter growing back in someone's hip. When I asked who it was, a woman stood up. She said that she had just met another woman who had fallen five years earlier and had broken her hip. After the fall the woman's hip never healed properly, leaving her in constant pain and confined to a wheelchair. Over the years, her condition got so bad that doctors scheduled surgery, which happened to be set for five days after our television taping.

Immediately I prayed for her health to be restored and for bone matter to grow in her hip. The woman in the studio audience then texted the other woman to tell her that we had prayed and she would be healed. When the woman read the text, she felt the power of God hit her. She then stood up and walked without pain for the first time in years!

Another miracle happened during that taping when I had a word about a breast mass getting softer. After I prayed, I asked everyone to check, and I saw a woman pressing hard all around her breast area. It was obvious by the look on her face that she had received a miracle. So I asked her to come up and share what happened. She said she'd had a golf-ball-sized growth in her breast that was extremely concerning. After the first day of our taping, however, she noticed that the growth got smaller. Once I prayed, it completely disappeared!

Stay With Grace

Your salvation was secured by grace through faith. Unfortunately, many Christians get saved and soon forget how important grace is. Thus many fail in their walk with God, get sick, and even die. We desperately need to hang on to grace and its power to heal and bring us victory.

The enemy will never quit accusing you of breaking the law. In fact he will stoop so low as to remind you of what Psalm 19:12 calls lapses, or hidden, unconscious faults. It's sad but true: Satan will accuse you of stuff you didn't even realize you were doing. Then he'll use it as legal ground to put death on you.

How do you stop this cycle? You stay in grace. If you keep going back to it, studying it, growing in it, and decreeing grace scriptures over yourself, the enemy won't find any opening through which to assault you. Grace will always superabound and fill every crack in your armor. That's why you must *never* stop trusting in God's grace.

Look at what Paul said about it:

> [Therefore, I do not treat God's gracious gift as something of minor importance and defeat its very purpose]; I do not set aside and invalidate and frustrate and nullify the grace (unmerited favor) of God. For if justification (righteousness, acquittal from guilt) comes through [observing the ritual of] the Law, then Christ (the Messiah) died groundlessly and to no purpose and in vain. [His death was then wholly superfluous.].
>
> —GALATIANS 2:21

The very purpose of grace is to trump the law. Again, to trump something means to gain an advantage over it. Thus, you should never nullify its power by setting it aside or diminishing its importance. Paul says that if you do that, you will be severed from Christ! Why would he say something so drastic? *Because if you believe that you can be justified and kept in right standing with God through your own strength, you don't need Christ or His sacrifice!*

That would be a punch in the face to our Lord, who was whipped, beaten, and pierced through with nine-inch nails so you could be declared righteous in God's sight. Galatians 5:4 echoes the same thought, saying, "If you seek to be justified and declared righteous and to be given a right standing with God through the Law, you are brought to nothing and so separated (severed) from Christ. You have fallen away from grace (from God's gracious favor and unmerited blessing)."

Do you know why you need to continue in grace? It's because you cannot keep the law! By His death, Christ fulfilled the righteous requirements of the law in you and for you. By grace He imparts this truth to you. So keep relying on grace. If you trust instead in your ability to keep the law, you will be severed from Christ and will consequently fall from grace!

Before you begin your grace activation, look at this: you are saved by grace through faith. Therefore faith is what activates God's grace in your life. But what if you lack the faith to believe that grace can do all it claims? Don't worry! Ephesians 2:8 says that faith is a gift, and Romans 12:3 says that everyone is given a measure of faith. Every believer starts out having some faith, and Jesus said it only takes faith the size of a mustard seed (one of the smallest seeds in the world) to move a mountain! (See Matthew 17:20.)

If you still think your faith is too small, grow it! Romans 10:17 says that "faith comes by hearing, and hearing by the word of God" (NKJV)! As you continue to study and decree grace scriptures, your faith to believe in grace will grow, and even more grace will be released into your life.

Grace Activation

Below are grace scriptures, many of which were already mentioned in this chapter. I encourage you to meditate on all of them. Use them to come against the enemy anytime you mess up or feel him assaulting you. As you declare that you are under grace and not the law, he will have to back off!

> For it is by free grace (God's unmerited favor) that you are saved (delivered from judgment and made partakers of Christ's salvation) through [your] faith. And this [salvation] is not of yourselves [of your own doing, it came not through your own striving], but it is the gift of God.
>
> —EPHESIANS 2:8

> For sin shall not [any longer] exert dominion over you, since now you are not under Law [as slaves], but under grace [as subjects of God's favor and mercy].
>
> —ROMANS 6:14

> But then Law came in, [only] to expand and increase the trespass [making it more apparent and exciting opposition]. But where sin increased and abounded, grace (God's unmerited favor) has surpassed it and increased the more and superabounded.
>
> —ROMANS 5:20

> [All] are justified and made upright and in right standing with God, freely and gratuitously by His grace (His unmerited favor and mercy), through the redemption which is [provided] in Christ Jesus.
>
> —ROMANS 3:24

> So that, [just] as sin has reigned in death, [so] grace (His unearned and undeserved favor) might reign also through righteousness (right standing with God) which issues in

eternal life through Jesus Christ (the Messiah, the Anointed One) our Lord.

—Romans 5:21

For out of His fullness (abundance) we have all received [all had a share and we were all supplied with] one grace after another and spiritual blessing upon spiritual blessing and even favor upon favor and gift [heaped] upon gift. For while the Law was given through Moses, grace (unearned, undeserved favor and spiritual blessing) and truth came through Jesus Christ.

—John 1:16–17

Through Him also we have [our] access (entrance, introduction) by faith into this grace (state of God's favor) in which we [firmly and safely] stand. And let us rejoice and exult in our hope of experiencing and enjoying the glory of God.

—Romans 5:2

But by the grace of God I am what I am, and his grace to me was not without effect. No, I worked harder than all of them— yet not I, but the grace of God that was with me.

—1 Corinthians 15:10, niv

Now Stephen, full of grace (divine blessing and favor) and power (strength and ability) worked great wonders and signs (miracles) among the people.

—Acts 6:8

Therefore, [inheriting] the promise is the outcome of faith and depends [entirely] on faith, in order that it might be given as an act of grace (unmerited favor), to make it stable and valid and guaranteed to all his descendants—not only to the devotees and adherents of the Law, but also to those who share the faith of Abraham, who is [thus] the father of us all...[For Abraham, human reason for] hope being gone, hoped in faith that he should become the father of many nations, as he had been promised, So [numberless] shall your descendants be. He did not weaken in faith when he considered the [utter] impotence of his own body, which was as good as dead because he was about a hundred years old, or [when he considered] the barrenness of Sarah's [deadened] womb. No unbelief or distrust made him waver (doubtingly question) concerning the promise of God, but he grew strong and was empowered by faith as he gave praise and glory to God.

—ROMANS 4:16, 18–20

Then [God] is gracious to him and says, Deliver him from going down into the pit [of destruction]; I have found a ransom (a price of redemption, an atonement)! [Then the man's] flesh shall be restored; it becomes fresher and more tender than a child's; he returns to the days of his youth.

—JOB 33:24–25

[Therefore, I do not treat God's gracious gift as something of minor importance and defeat its very purpose]; I do not set aside and invalidate and frustrate and nullify the grace (unmerited favor) of God. For if justification (righteousness, acquittal from guilt) comes through [observing the ritual of] the Law, then Christ (the Messiah) died groundlessly and to no purpose and in vain. [His death was then wholly superfluous.]

—GALATIANS 2:21

Grace Decrees

Make the following decrees and repeat them as needed. They are based in Scripture and will encourage your faith.

Lord, I decree that although I have sinned by breaking Your laws, sin no longer has dominion over me, because of grace. I decree that I am no longer under the law as a slave but am under grace as a subject of Your favor and mercy.

I decree that when my sins of lawbreaking increase and abound, grace (God's unmerited favor) has surpassed them and increased the more and even superabounded over them.

I decree that I am justified and made upright and in right standing with God, freely and gratuitously, by His grace (His unmerited favor and mercy). This is accomplished only through Jesus and not through my keeping of the law.

I decree that just as sin enabled death to reign over me, His grace (unearned and undeserved favor) is reigning in me through righteousness and right standing with God.

I decree that out of His fullness I am constantly being supplied with one grace after another. Spiritual blessing upon spiritual blessing, favor upon favor, and gift upon gift are being heaped on me.

I decree that I have access by faith into this grace (state of God's favor) in which I firmly and safely stand. Thus I rejoice and exult in hope!

I decree that God's grace is effectual in my life. I am able to work harder, do more, and be more effective for my family, friends, and the kingdom because of God's grace working in me! I also decree that grace has the power to heal my body of any injury or brush with death, just as it did for Paul.

I decree that I am like Stephen, who was full of grace and power and worked great wonders, signs, and miracles among the people.

I decree that I share the faith of Abraham, who is the father of us all. Therefore I will inherit all God's promises, through faith, so that they may be given as acts of grace and not through my adherence to the law. Like Abraham, I will not weaken in faith but will believe for my youth to be totally restored, even if my body is in a completely deadened state. No unbelief or distrust will make me waver or doubtingly question God's promise, but I will grow strong in faith as I give praise and glory to Him.

I decree that God has found an atoning sacrifice for me in Jesus, and through His grace my flesh shall be restored. I believe that my skin is becoming fresher than a child's and I am returning to the days of my youth. I decree that my fat flesh is being removed and I am returning to the size I was in the days of my youth. I decree that my lean flesh is getting firmer and my muscles are growing stronger. I decree that I am being revived from sterility and that all my reproductive systems are returning to their youthful state. I decree that I am fresh and young looking and feeling great! I am fertile and not barren. I am not suffering from any menopausal symptoms, and no matter how far gone my body might be, I will return to the days of my youth because of Christ's atoning work and His grace!

I decree that from this moment on I will not treat God's gracious gift as something of minor importance and thereby defeat its very purpose. I will not set it aside and invalidate, frustrate, or nullify it. Thus I will never be separated from Christ, and I will never fall from grace. I will continue in grace so that Satan has no right to accuse me of breaking the law. Therefore death's attack on my life will be destroyed!

Healing Commands

1. I command my soul be healed of trauma, in Jesus' name.

2. I command all curses to break, in Jesus' name.

3. I command all spirits of infirmity to go, in Jesus' name.

4. I bind death's action on my bodily organs, in Jesus' name. (List your organs and bind death off each one.)

5. I command disease, bacteria, and viruses to die, in Jesus' name.

6. I command all pain to go and the root cause of it to be healed, in Jesus' name.

7. I ask the Spirit of life to be released into every organ in my body and every part of my frame, from head to toe

(including bones, blood, tissues, organs, etc.), in Jesus' name.

Now, to see if your breakthrough has occurred, test yourself by doing something you couldn't do before. Don't forget to send us your two-minute selfie video of your miracle testimony. (Be sure to hold your phone in the landscape position.) Email your video to selfies@katiesouza.com.

Return to this chapter often to remind yourself that God's grace is working on your behalf.

CHAPTER 4

SATAN THE LEGALIST

SATAN IS ABLE to use the law against us because he knows *no one* can keep it perfectly (Jas. 2:10–11). He is the ultimate prosecuting attorney, constantly using the commandments as his tool to bring a death sentence against you.

The name Satan in the New Testament is from the Greek word *Satanas*, which means "accuser."[1] The devil comes to steal, kill, and destroy (John 10:10), and he accomplishes these goals through non-stop indictments concerning your lawbreaking. Revelation 12:10 says he accuses the brethren before God "day and night." The Greek word translated "accuser" is *katēgoreō*, which means "to be a plaintiff... to charge with some offence."[2]

That's Satan all right, constantly charging you with breaking the law. Here's the rub: he does more than whisper condemning thoughts into your mind and speak horrible things about you to others. He brings formal charges against you so he can obtain a verdict of death and release it over your life.

Allegations have no binding ramifications of punishment unless they are presented in court. *Katēgoreō* ("accuser") has a court-related definition meaning "to make an accusation," specifically "before a judge."[3] Satan always charges you in the presence of a judge—and not some random justice of the peace either. Satan takes his case to the judge of all the earth, who presides over the highest courts in the universe: the courts of heaven.

The Courts of Heaven

As I proceed into this revelation on the courts of heaven, let me first start by saying that I did not birth this powerful insight. Rather, Robert Henderson and others are the "fathers" of this teaching. I encourage you to research the resources they offer on this topic. However, God has given me my own insights that powerfully connect the courts of the Lord with defeating death. As you will see, you cannot succeed in obtaining restored youth for your body unless you are operating in the courts.

Do the courts of heaven actually exist? The Bible indicates a firm *yes*. First of all, Scripture calls God "the Judge of all the earth" (Gen. 18:25, ESV). Isaiah yokes God's role as judge with that of lawgiver, writing, "The LORD is our judge, the LORD is our lawgiver" (Isa. 33:22, KJV). The titles go hand in hand because the same God who created the law also enforces it.

The judge of all the earth serves as chief justice from His bench in the eternal realm. His laws are evident in His Word but are also actively enforced from the courts of heaven. Here's what Scripture says: *"You caused judgment to be heard from heaven*; the earth feared and was still, when God arose to judgment, to deliver all the oppressed of the earth. Selah"* (Ps. 76:8–9, NKJV).

The Amplified Bible, Classic Edition says that God causes His "sentence to be heard from heaven" so the oppressed can be delivered (Ps. 76:8–9). Heaven's verdicts supersede every earthly verdict, even those issued from the highest courts. I have experienced firsthand what it's like to be sentenced in a governmental court of law. I know how binding those judgments are; the consequences and punishments are far-reaching. I was sentenced to twelve-and-a-half-years in federal prison. However, when God brought His righteous justice from heaven's court, my prison time was reduced to less than five years!

God continually releases His rulings into the earth and into our personal lives. The prophet Daniel saw this process firsthand.

> I kept looking until thrones were placed [for the assessors with the Judge], and the Ancient of Days [God, the eternal

Father] took His seat, Whose garment was white as snow and the hair of His head like pure wool. His throne was like the fiery flame; its wheels were burning fire. A stream of fire came forth from before Him; a thousand thousands ministered to Him and ten thousand times ten thousand rose up and stood before Him; the Judge was seated [the court was in session] and the books were opened.

—DANIEL 7:9–10

Earthly courts pale in comparison to the fearsome, awe-inspiring, raw power that is present when the Ancient of Days takes His seat in the courts of heaven. The stream of fire coming from His throne represents the fiery judgments of God being released into the earth. The gravity of the decision Daniel witnessed in the following verse was of such magnitude that Jesus Himself was called to the witness stand:

Behold, on the clouds of the heavens came One like a Son of man, and He came to the Ancient of Days and was presented before Him.

—DANIEL 7:13

Jesus' testimony decreed that His sacrifice on the cross would produce eternal dominion for the Son of God and His elect. Christ and the church will have total dominion in the earth forever *because* of this pronouncement made in the court of the Ancient of Days:

There was given Him [the Messiah] dominion and glory and kingdom, that all peoples, nations, and languages should serve Him. His dominion is an everlasting dominion which shall not pass away, and His kingdom is one which shall not be destroyed.... The saints of the Most High [God] shall receive the kingdom and possess the kingdom forever, even forever and ever.

—DANIEL 7:14, 18

Remember, no decision can be legally enforced unless it is executed in the courts of heaven. Satan knows this. Therefore he doesn't waste his time accusing you informally. Rather, he brings all his charges into court so he can obtain a legal and effectual verdict against you and ensure that the penalty of death is incurred and paid.

Satan in the Courts

Satan was thrown out of heaven long ago. He no longer resides there but still has access to heaven's courts so he can bring charges against you. Let's look at some of the many biblical examples of this:

> Now there was a day when the sons of God came to present themselves before the LORD, and Satan also came among them. And the LORD said to Satan, "From where do you come?"
>
> So Satan answered the LORD and said, "From going to and fro on the earth, and from walking back and forth on it."
>
> Then the LORD said to Satan, "Have you considered My servant Job, that there is none like him on the earth, a blameless and upright man, one who fears God and shuns evil?"
>
> So Satan answered the LORD and said, "Does Job fear God for nothing? Have You not made a hedge around him, around his household, and around all that he has on every side? You have blessed the work of his hands, and his possessions have increased in the land. But now, stretch out Your hand and touch all that he has, and he will surely curse You to Your face!"
>
> —JOB 1:6–11, NKJV

When Satan appeared before God that day, he immediately brought accusations against Job, which proves that the scene occurred in a heavenly courtroom. Satan charged that Job only loved and feared God because God had blessed and protected him. Satan went as far as to claim that if God lifted His hedge of protection from around Job, His servant would curse Him to His face.

Those are some serious allegations. If you know the story, you're also aware that one of Satan's goals in filing this lawsuit was to legally put the spirit of death on Job's life! He succeeded in this by killing all of Job's servants and his children while also putting a painful disease on Job's body! When Satan charges you in court, he always makes death part of your punishment. You can see that through the tragedies Job endured.

What enables the enemy to win his case against you? He presents evidence of your guilt to the court. Notice that when God asked Satan, "From where do you come?" Satan replied, "From going to and fro on the earth, and from walking back and forth on it" (Job 1:7, NKJV). The phrase "from going to and fro" is from the Hebrew word *shuwt*, which metaphorically means "*to run through a book*," i.e. to examine thoroughly."[4] In other words, Satan came to court prepared!

Daniel 7 says that when the court convened, "the books were opened" (Dan. 7:10, NKJV). Entire books in heaven are filled with the record of events that happened on the earth, and some of the books include the details of your life. (See Revelation 3:5.) Satan continually scours the world for proof of your guilt so he can enter it into the court's records and use it against you.

When I was first taken into the courts of heaven, I was shown a room where Satan stored evidence he had gathered for a case against me. The room was stuffed with old metal filing cabinets overflowing with files and documents of every kind. Stacked on top of the cabinets were more boxes, files, and documents. Paperwork was strewn everywhere. When I asked the Holy Spirit what I was seeing, He said it was evidence of every single time I broke the law. Shortly after seeing this, I was visited by the spirit of death!

Satan is a legalist. The number-one weapon he uses against you is your lawbreaking. He will use any and every transgression against you in court, even what the Bible calls your "hidden" and "unconscious" faults (Ps. 19:12). Absolutely no one is exempt from his accusations. He even brought a case against the high priest Joshua.

> Then he showed me Joshua the high priest standing before the Angel of the LORD, and Satan standing at his right hand to oppose him. And the LORD said to Satan, "The LORD rebuke you, Satan! The LORD who has chosen Jerusalem rebuke you! Is this not a brand plucked from the fire?"

Now Joshua was clothed with filthy garments, and was standing before the Angel.

Then He answered and spoke to those who stood before Him, saying, "Take away the filthy garments from him." And to him He said, "See, I have removed your iniquity from you, and I will clothe you with rich robes."

And I said, "Let them put a clean turban on his head."

So they put a clean turban on his head, and they put the clothes on him. And the Angel of the LORD stood by.

Then the Angel of the LORD admonished Joshua, saying, "Thus says the LORD of hosts: 'If you will walk in My ways, and if you will keep My command, then you shall also judge My house, and likewise have charge of My courts; I will give you places to walk among these who stand here.'"

—ZECHARIAH 3:1–7, NKJV

Again, an accusation holds no power unless it is presented in court. Then and only then will it produce a verdict authorizing the accuser to execute the punishment prescribed by the sentence. The scene in which Satan accused Joshua is courtroom drama at its best. The Israelites had just returned to Jerusalem after seventy years of captivity in Babylon and were trying desperately to rebuild the temple. We see Satan *standing* at Joshua's right hand and pointing to his filthy clothes, which represented his sin. The word translated "standing" is *'amad*, which means "*to impose* (a law) on anyone."[5]

Satan's goal in this trial was to try to stop the completion of the new temple by accusing Joshua of breaking the law. The devil's intentions for you are the same. He wants to stop you from rebuilding *your* temple, which is your body! Thus he will go into court armed with files of your lawbreaking so he can put death on your body. However, remember that Zerubbabel finished his work on the temple when the people shouted, "Grace, grace," to that mountain of resistance (Zech. 4:7).

Grace will win your case. The lawsuit filed against Joshua was so important that the Angel of the Lord was present in court to rebuke Satan on Joshua's behalf! Why? Many theologians believe this was

Christ Himself who would become the atoning sacrifice for all mankind. Because of the presence of the Lord, God not only took away Joshua's sin but dressed him in robes of righteousness that he didn't deserve. This is a perfect picture of the unearned, unmerited grace of God triumphing over the law!

It is interesting that once Joshua was found innocent on all counts, the Angel of the Lord told him he would judge God's people and keep charge of the Lord's courts! This is what happens when you operate in grace. You are cleared of all indictments and freed to administrate justice on behalf of others, including those who have the spirit of death attacking their bodily organs.

My friend Doug Addison mentioned this story about Joshua when he prophesied that I was going to have an office in the courts. In studying Joshua, I found that he was one of the Israelites held in captivity in Babylon and then was chosen to be the high priest during the reconstruction of the temple when the Israelites returned from captivity. (See Zechariah 6:9–14 and Ezra 3.) Like Joshua, I did time in prison. So until grace came, we were both brands plucked from the fire, dressed in filthy garments, and accused by Satan. As He did for Joshua, however, the Lord gave me clean robes of righteousness that I didn't deserve. He did this through His grace. Because I have been declared innocent, I now have the authority in His courts to break the spirit of death off of people's lives so their temples can be rebuilt.

New Testament Courts

The Gospels contain more proof of Satan's courtroom activity. In the Book of Luke, Satan demanded that Peter be tried for the sins he was about to commit by betraying Jesus. Jesus revealed Satan's accusation to Peter:

> The Lord said, Simon, Simon, behold, Satan hath desired to have you, that he may sift you as wheat: but I have prayed

> for thee, that thy faith fail not: and when thou art converted,
> strengthen thy brethren.
>
> —Luke 22:31–32, kjv

The word translated "desired" in verse 31 is *exaiteō*, which means "to demand (for trial)."[6] The word also suggests being subjected "for torture, for punishment."[7] Satan wanted to take Peter to trial so he could accuse him of sin and obtain a legal verdict to have him tortured and punished for betraying Jesus.

This is a New Testament example of what Satan is doing to all believers today. He's constantly roaming to and fro on the earth, searching for evidence of your lawbreaking so he can present it in court and receive legal authority to torture and punish you through pain, disease, sickness, poverty, and even death.

I love how Jesus said He was praying for Peter so that when Peter overcame, he could "strengthen" his brethren (Luke 22:32). The Greek word translated "strengthen" is *stērizō*,[8] which is believed to be from the root word *histēmi*, meaning "to cause or make to stand" as "before judges."[9] Just as Joshua was given charge of the courts after his acquittal, so was Peter. When grace superabounded over his sin, he won the case Satan brought against him, then he returned to strengthen his brethren just as he had been strengthened.

Once you win your case through God's grace, you can help your fellow believers stand up to Satan, get their rights in heaven's courts, and defeat the spirit of death.

You Must Face Your Enemy in Court

Did you know that whoever doesn't show up for a court case loses? That's why Jesus prayed for Peter when He found out Satan had demanded he be taken to trial. If Jesus has not gone to court on Peter's behalf, then he would have lost his case. While on the street, I was arrested many times for lawbreaking. Often I got bailed out based on my promise to show up for a later hearing to decide my guilt or innocence. However, I always failed to show up, so the court would immediately issue a warrant for my arrest, and the police would take me into custody.

Moral of the story: whoever doesn't show up for court loses! You must go to court and face Satan's charges, or you will lose your case against death! God directs all believers to show up by saying, "Put Me in remembrance [remind Me of your merits]; let us plead and argue together. Set forth your case, that you may be justified (proved right)" (Isa. 43:26).

You need not fear going to court even if you are guilty of breaking the law. It is by grace through faith that you are justified and proven righteous! As you step into court, releasing repentance and grace, the blood Jesus shed on your behalf will enable you to receive a "not guilty" verdict every single time.

Look again at Revelation 12:

> Then I heard a strong (loud) voice in heaven, saying, Now it has come—the salvation and the power and the kingdom (the dominion, the reign) of our God, and the power (the sovereignty, the authority) of His Christ (the Messiah); for the accuser of our brethren, he who keeps bringing before our God charges against them day and night, has been cast out! And they have overcome (conquered) him by means of the blood of the Lamb and by the utterance of their testimony.
>
> —REVELATION 12:10–11

Again, the Greek word for *accuser* involves making an accusation "before a judge."[10] Satan is the prosecuting attorney. He never gets tired of bringing charges against you, by day or by night. The good news is that he has been cast down, and this passage tells how! Any Christian can conquer and overcome him through "the blood of the Lamb and...the utterance of their testimony"!

You must go into court and *testify* about the power of the blood and grace to cleanse you of every sin for which Satan accuses you. When you take the witness stand and testify of Christ's work on the cross, you proclaim before the entire court that through the shedding of His blood,

Jesus has fulfilled the righteous requirements of the law on your behalf. Therefore the sentence of death against you must be revoked!

Jesus Instructs Us to Take the Spirit of Death to Court

Believe it or not, there is a story in the New Testament that proves Jesus wants you to take the spirit of death to court. It is the story of the persistent widow.

> Also [Jesus] told them a parable to the effect that they ought always to pray and not to turn coward (faint, lose heart, and give up). He said, In a certain city there was a judge who neither reverenced and feared God nor respected or considered man. And there was a widow in that city who kept coming to him and saying, Protect and defend and give me justice against my adversary. And for a time he would not; but later he said to himself, Though I have neither reverence or fear for God nor respect or consideration for man, yet because this widow continues to bother me, I will defend and protect and avenge her, lest she give me intolerable annoyance and wear me out by her continual coming or at the last she come and rail on me or assault me or strangle me. Then the Lord said, Listen to what the unjust judge says! And will not [our just] God defend and protect and avenge His elect (His chosen ones), who cry to Him day and night? Will He defer them and delay help on their behalf? I tell you, He will defend and protect and avenge them speedily. However, when the Son of Man comes, will He find [persistence in] faith on the earth?
>
> —LUKE 18:1–8

Here Jesus used the parable of a widow and an earthly judge to show the importance of standing against the enemy and seeking justice against death *in the courts*. The persistent widow asked the unjust judge for justice against her "adversary." The Greek word is *antidikos*, which means "an opponent (in a lawsuit); specially, Satan"![11] Because Jesus told this story as a parable, it suggests that the principle applies to every believer. He is our courtroom opponent, and we must be as persistent as the widow—not only to appear before the judge but to appear repeatedly until we get the justice we need!

What kind of judgment was the widow pursuing? Because she was suddenly left completely alone, I'm sure she needed many things. However, because of the language in this passage, I am convinced that she also wanted a ruling against the spirit of death! The King James Version says that she asked the judge to "avenge" her of her "adversary" (Luke 18:3, KJV). The Greek word translated "avenge" is *ekdikeō*, which means "to demand in punishment, the blood of one from another, i.e. *to exact of the murderer the penalty of his crime.*"[12]

Satan is a murderer! He comes to steal, kill, and destroy!

He had attacked the widow's house. The very definition of the word *widow* is a woman who has lost her spouse *by death*! Her husband had been killed by that deadly spirit! Now she was out for blood because her precious spouse was gone and with him, her companionship, protection, and provision. She wanted that murdering devil to pay for his crime, which is why she was unceasing in seeking justice from the court! Plus she may have been getting old herself, in which case the spirit of death would have afflicted her body with many painful problems. I'm certain the same evil spirit that took her husband was also stalking her and trying to take her life too!

The widow wanted justice against her enemy, and the unjust judge gave it to her! He said, "I will *avenge* her, lest by her continual coming she weary me" (v. 5, KJV). The word *avenge* indicates that the unjust judge gave her exactly what she wanted. He exacted from that murderer the penalty for his crime, and the widow finally received her justice.

When I was battling the spirit of death, the fight stretched over a two-and-a-half-year span, during which my body was viciously attacked, as I mentioned in chapter 2. However, that was just a part of the massive destruction the devil wrought on our lives. The enemy attacked people who were very close to me, and his assault led to their deaths. Some were like family, including my senior prayer general and close friend,

Georgia Marshall. The unborn child of my other close friend and prayer intercessor died. Then our precious dogs, Bandit and Luke, who were like our children, died within two weeks of each other! After that the enemy tried to create major strife in our marriage of fifteen years. It was the fiercest, most exhausting, and painful battle of our lives! (That was when I discovered that the enemy had filed a divorce decree in heaven's court to split us up.)

After that Satan and death went after the ministry, tearing it apart. Our relationships with our vendors developed into some of the most challenging ones my team had ever dealt with. I also lost four valuable and trusted employees. The ones who remained were so loaded with responsibility that it wore them down. Some were close to quitting.

Satan even raised up leaders to criticize and judge me and sent spirits to torment me nightly in my body and mind and to beat me down while I was on tour. During that time, I hardly slept and was totally exhausted. Finally I became completely burned out and extremely discouraged.

To say I was out for blood is an understatement! I became the persistent widow, going into the courts over and over again, seeking to be avenged of my enemy. I wanted that murderer to pay for his crimes. The process was agonizing, as all court cases are, but we got our justice! Step by step, everything was restored. The Lord brought peace to and unity in our marriage. My health went into an upswing as I slowly watched my body return to the days of my youth.

The ministry was also supernaturally blessed with the people and services we needed to grow bigger and stronger than we had ever been before. We began to receive unusual favor with other churches and prisons across the country. We also launched into a whole new realm of social media broadcasting and exploded in growth and finances as a result. As for the people we lost to death, this world is not the same without them. But now they are in the great cloud of witnesses, *testifying* for us in heaven's courts. They are even more effective than they could possibly have been here on earth!

Power Over Death

After I won the cases Satan brought against me, I discovered that I had authority to remove the spirit of death from others. I was ministering in a meeting in Minnesota when I felt a tug on the back of my shirt. I turned to see a tiny woman who looked very ill. Her name was Marilyn. She had persistently waited for me to pray for her and was not going to leave until I did. When I asked her how I could help, she exclaimed, "My body is dying!"

She then told me that she had contracted an extreme case of mold poisoning along with radon poisoning. Even after she was treated, her body could not recover. As she continued to tell her story, I couldn't help but notice how frail she was. She looked like a skeleton. Her bones were sticking out, and her skin was dark and gray in color. She quite literally looked like death warmed over. As she described how much she'd suffered, it was easy to understand her appearance. She was unable to eat, couldn't stand up, could not lift her hands to drive her car, and was unable to open doors. She had no strength whatsoever.

Then, as she was speaking, something strange happened. I saw a vision of myself violently shaking her while commanding the spirit of death to come out. When she paused, I said, "I just saw myself doing something pretty extreme to you. Are you OK if I do it?"

She immediately cried, "Yes! Do whatever you need to do! I came here to get healed!"

So I grabbed her, shook her violently, and shouted, "Death, come out!"

I did this six or seven times, after which she dropped to the floor, crying. I panicked, thinking I had hurt her. But while she lay there, I asked the Spirit of life to flow into her body and bring life to every place she needed it.

When she was done crying, I asked, "What happened?"

Looking wide-eyed at her daughter, she said, "Did you see that?"

Her daughter said, "No, what?"

She replied, "That big puff of black smoke that came out of me as I went down!"

Marilyn had been delivered of the spirit of death.

The next day, as I finished speaking, a beautiful, polished-looking woman walked up to the platform. Suddenly I realized it was Marilyn. It had been less than twenty-four hours, and she already looked amazing! She glowed as she told me that she had awakened full of energy and had gotten dressed with no trouble. She was also delighted to discover that as she and her family walked through the parking lot and into the church, she walked faster than all of them. She also danced during the entire morning worship and even ate a whole sandwich for lunch.

Like the persistent widow in Luke 18, Marilyn had been avenged of her enemy, the spirit of death. Her parting words to me were "I knew I came [to this meeting] so I could live!" You can watch Marilyn's testimony at the link provided in the notes.[13]

Keys to Winning in Court!

The persistent widow received her restitution. Let's look at keys to winning your case too.

First, like I said earlier, you must show up in court! Whoever doesn't show up loses their claim. The persistent widow not only presented herself before the unjust judge once but appeared repeatedly until he gave her the justice she was seeking. She was shameless and confident in her petition, knowing that she would receive a righteous verdict. Because of Jesus, you can have the same confidence to go "boldly to the throne of grace... [to] obtain mercy and find grace in [your] time of need" (Heb. 4:16, NKJV).

Second, you have to realize that during your case, your faith will be tested. Just keep praying and petitioning. Do not lose heart while awaiting your verdict. That was the point of Jesus' parable in the first place. He was preparing His disciples to always "pray and not... turn coward (faint, lose heart, and give up)" (Luke 18:1). Justice takes time. Court cases in earthly systems can drag on for years and even decades. Heaven's courts are typically much faster, but the judicial process must take place. You might get your verdict the same day, or you may have to wait longer.

Why is that? And why does the story of the persistent widow seem to reveal contradictions? On one hand, Jesus said to always pray and not give up, indicating that patience would be needed. But at the end of the story He said this:

> Will not [our just] God defend and protect and avenge His elect (His chosen ones), who cry to Him day and night? Will He defer them and delay help on their behalf? I tell you, He will defend and protect and avenge them speedily.
>
> —LUKE 18:7–8

So which is it? Do you need to patiently pray and not give up, or is God going to avenge you speedily?

It's both! Jesus asks you to pray not because God is reluctant but because He isn't! This is your encouragement to continue praying! God is not like the unjust judge. You can pray confidently and not give up *because* you know God will answer your prayers speedily! If you face delays, just remember this: prayer is not meant to change God but to transform you. Persistence in prayer builds in you the character of God Himself.

Heaven's courts administer justice more quickly than courts on earth, but while you wait, you need to stay persistent in your faith—praying, trusting, worshipping, and leaning into God's Word. Look at Jesus' exhortation in the parable of the persistent widow: "However, when the Son of Man comes, will He find [persistence in] faith on the earth?" (Luke 18:8). I have heard people say that if you pray more than once, you don't have faith. Yet here Jesus says to persist in your faith. Whenever I lack confidence for something to happen, I keep praying into it until I receive the gift of faith to believe that it is done.

The third key I want to mention involves your words. I learned the hard way that sin will delay your verdict. This is especially true when you sin with your mouth. During our battle with death, I faced extreme challenges. Satan pulled out all the stops trying to get me tired, offended, judgmental, and critical. Many times I just wanted to give up and even quit the ministry. Out of all the bad decisions I made during that time, the worst was that I let myself get angry and offended and then run my mouth.

During your court case, Satan will wreak havoc in your life. His goal is to get you so frazzled that you start sinning in your mind and emotions and with your mouth. Every time you judge or criticize someone or complain about your situation, Satan records every word as evidence against you and files a brand-new case to delay the first one!

Look at what Jesus says in this eye-opening verse: "By your words you will be acquitted, and by your words you will be condemned" (Matt. 12:37, NIV). Satan *constantly* uses your words to file new court claims to slow down your ability to receive justice. In the battle against death the stakes are high. Your biggest challenge will be to bite your tongue and keep quiet, no matter what anyone says or does to you! Doug Addison had a word from the Lord about this once. He said he saw the courts totally clogged up with cases filed by believers who were bringing suits against each other through their judgmental words!

I believe one of the reasons Job's battle dragged on for so long is because he complained a lot! The Book of Job records him as saying all kinds of crazy stuff because of the pain he endured at the enemy's hands. Don't get me wrong. I have total compassion for Job, and the Bible makes it clear that he was not suffering because of sin in his life. Satan took everything from him, including his children and his wealth. He afflicted Job with painful boils, directed his friends to fight him, and even caused his wife to turn against him. Job had plenty to complain about! But it wasn't until Job stopped complaining and looked to the Lord for revelation that He experienced a breakthrough. Job said, "I have heard of You by the hearing of the ear; but now my eye sees You; therefore I retract, and I repent in dust and ashes" (Job 42:5–6, NASB).

Satan wants us to focus so much on what he is doing that we fail to turn our attention to God. Instead we focus on the pain and the problems. That is exactly what Satan counts on! So many believers never get answers to their prayers because while they wait for justice, the warfare drives them to talk smack. Don't forget what Matthew 12:37 says: you will be judged or acquitted by every word you say. This is true even if your suffering seems unfair.

Whenever the enemy tries to torment me and get me to complain, I just start praising and thanking God. First Thessalonians 5:16–18 says, "Rejoice always, pray without ceasing, give thanks in all circumstances" (ESV). No matter what horrible situation Satan puts on you, rejoice your way through it. I believe that will cut your battle and wait time in half! This is crucial when you're fighting death. You can easily get discouraged when your body weakens, your sickness gets worse, your appearance ages, and your belly enlarges. But complaining about it will only delay your victory! Stay thankful during the battle. The sacrifice is worth it!

Heaven's Court Activation

In the next chapter, I will show you the specific court that specializes in defeating the spirit of death. Every believer has access to this court. It's the grace court. For now, prepare to enter His court of grace by making the following decrees:

Lord, my adversary and opponent at law, Satan, has been going to and fro upon the earth gathering evidence of my guilt to present before You in court. Night and day he accuses me of breaking the law so he can secure a guilty verdict against me and ensure the sentence of death. So, Lord, I announce my intent to appear in court before You, the judge of all the earth, to face the charges against me. Like the persistent widow, I will be shameless and bold in coming before You, my righteous judge. I will have the same confidence she had and will appear in court as many times as needed until my case is decided and finalized! I know I will be avenged and will see those murderers (Satan and death) pay the penalty for their crimes.

While I wait for my case to be settled, I will keep praying not to give up or lose heart. Jesus said the Father is not like the unjust judge who deferred judgment for the widow. Instead Jesus asked, "Will not God give justice to his elect, who cry to him day and night?" (Luke 18:7, ESV). I believe the Lord will not withhold or delay His help on my behalf but will defend, protect, and avenge me speedily.

While I wait for my sure victory, I will not let the traumatic circumstances Satan puts on me to cause me to complain, gossip, judge, or criticize people. Instead I will rejoice always and give thanks in every difficult circumstance. If I slip up, I will immediately repent so that Satan cannot use my words to open a new case against me and thus delay my righteous verdict!

I decree all these things in Jesus' name. Amen!

CHAPTER 5

THE GRACE COURT

I N THE WORLD there are many different categories of courts. A few examples are civil, criminal, and family courts, and in the United States there is the Supreme Court. Everything on earth is fashioned after the governmental pattern of heaven. Like earth the eternal realm has different courts of law, one of which is the grace court. The writer of Hebrews wrote,

> Let us therefore come boldly to the throne of grace, that we may obtain mercy and find grace to help in time of need.
> —HEBREWS 4:16, NKJV

The Greek word for *throne* in this verse is *thronos*.[1] It is a "seat" used by kings or judges that is "equivalent to [a] tribunal or bench."[2] (See also Matthew 19:28; Luke 22:30; and Revelation 20:4.) The throne in Hebrews 4 is not just a chair that God sits on. Rather, it is the bench from which the judge of all the earth releases justice and mercy for His people through His glorious grace!

Have you ever heard the expression "throw yourself on the mercy of the court"? That's what happens in this courtroom. Here all decisions and rulings are based on the grace and mercy of God. If you keep your heart from being hardened by sin to the point of unrepentance, you cannot fail in the grace court. The Bible says that "mercy triumphs over judgment" (Jas. 2:13, NKJV), and grace *always* trumps the law. Hence in this court you can never lose!

Even (and especially) when fighting the spirit of death, the grace court is where you present your case. Death obtained its legal right to attack your bodily organs through your lawbreaking. However, where sin abounds, grace superabounds! Every judgment that death put on your body will have to bow its knee in God's court of grace. The best news is that *any believer* can *boldly* enter this court to receive grace and mercy in their time of need.

The Grace Court and Youth

Don't forget: grace is how Abraham and Sarah experienced renewed youth so they could birth the promised child, Isaac. Let's look at Romans 4:16 again:

> Therefore, [inheriting] the promise is the outcome of faith and depends [entirely] on faith, in order that it might be given as an act of grace (unmerited favor), to make it stable and valid and guaranteed to all his descendants—not only to the devotees and adherents of the Law, but also to those who share the faith of Abraham, who is [thus] the father of us all.

You inherit the promises by grace through faith, not through your ability to keep the law. As you bring your case against death into the grace court, you will win a righteous judgment and see death's power over your life destroyed.

Now notice that the Bible connects grace and the courts with astounding youth-renewing scriptures. Look at these amazing examples, beginning with Psalm 92:

> The [uncompromisingly] righteous shall flourish like the palm tree [be long-lived, stately, upright, useful, and fruitful]; they shall grow like a cedar in Lebanon [majestic, stable, durable, and incorruptible]. Planted in the house of the Lord, *they shall flourish in the courts of our God. [Growing in grace] they shall still bring forth fruit in old age*; they shall be full of sap [of spiritual vitality] and [rich in the] verdure [of trust, love, and contentment].
>
> —PSALM 92:12–14

This psalm promises that you can be long-lived like a palm tree, incorruptible and durable as a cedar, and able to bring forth fruit in your old age. Notice that these things happen when you "flourish in the courts of our God. [Growing in grace]"!

How do you do that? Faith comes by hearing and hearing by the Word of God. As you continue to study scriptures concerning grace and the courts, you will grow and flourish in both. Personally I make sure that certain revelations (including those involving grace and the courts) never fall by the wayside. Because I have pursued deeper understanding concerning both these biblical topics, I have developed greater levels of authority, influence, and success over the years. I believe you will also prosper and increase immensely as you continue to grow in grace and flourish in His courts.

One of the most powerful youth-restoring promises in the Bible is directly connected to getting justice in the courts. Take a look:

> Bless the LORD, O my soul; and all that is within me, bless His holy name! Bless the LORD, O my soul, and forget not all His benefits: who forgives all your iniquities, who heals all your diseases, who redeems your life from destruction, who crowns you with lovingkindness and tender mercies, who satisfies your mouth with good things, so that your youth is renewed like the eagle's.
>
> —PSALM 103:1–5, NKJV

Most Christians have set their hopes on this soul-healing, disease-breaking, youth-restoring psalm at one time or another. Yet very few have connected the promises in verses 1–5 with the one in verse 6: "The LORD executes righteousness and justice for all who are oppressed" (NKJV). The word translated "justice" here is courtroom language. It's the Hebrew word *mishpât*, which indicates "a verdict...pronounced judicially."[3] It is no coincidence that immediately after promising to heal your diseases and renew your youth, God promises to execute a verdict for you in court. I believe it proves that part of God's justice for His people is disease-destroying, youth-regenerating power!

Mishpât also means "to plead any one's cause" and is "used of that which is lawfully due to any one."[4] This means God is pleading your case to make sure you get what is lawfully due you in His Word! The death sentence Satan enforces for your lawbreaking will be overturned in God's grace court, thus you will be issued what the Bible promises—power for your youth to be renewed!

Grace and the courts are also connected to the promise that says your flesh will become fresher than a child's. Remember that passage in Job? It began with the man who was close to death. He was in constant pain, with his flesh wasting away and his bones sticking out. Yet God's atoning sacrifice and grace returned him to the days of his youth. Look again at this amazing miracle promise:

> Then [God] is gracious to him and says, Deliver him from going down into the pit [of destruction]; I have found a ransom (a price of redemption, an atonement)! [Then the man's] flesh shall be restored; it becomes fresher and more tender than a child's; he returns to the days of his youth.
>
> —JOB 33:24–25

Because of Jesus' atoning sacrifice, you can experience this kind of miracle in your body. As you learned earlier, this youth renewal includes the regeneration of your skin and the rebalancing of fat and lean flesh. The Scriptures even promise that you can be revived from sterility. But now look closely at the very next verse because it connects the manifestation of this promise to His grace and the courts: "He {the dying man already described} shall pray to God, and He will delight in him, he shall see His face with joy, *for He restores to man His righteousness*" (Job 33:26, NKJV).

The word for *righteousness* here is *tsĕdaqah*, which means "justice...in freeing, vindicating, and rewarding the godly."[5] Justice for the godly is dispensed in the grace court. This verse states that God restored to that man *His* righteousness. We are made righteous by grace through faith in Jesus Christ! The grace court is where God declares you to be what Jesus won for you: you are justified and righteous and in right standing with God. Renewed youth is part of the just verdict you receive because of Christ's all-atoning sacrifice and His grace.

Now let me share one of the most quoted youth-restoring passages in Scripture. You have seen part of it already, but I will show you now how it is also connected to the courts.

> Have you not known? Have you not heard? The everlasting God, the LORD, the Creator of the ends of the earth, neither faints nor is weary. His understanding is unsearchable. He gives power to the weak, and to those who have no might He increases strength. Even the youths shall faint and be weary, and the young men shall utterly fall, but those who wait on the LORD shall renew their strength; they shall mount up with wings like eagles, they shall run and not be weary, they shall walk and not faint.
>
> —ISAIAH 40:28–31, NKJV

The word for *might* is *'own,* which means "strength, power...specially of virile and genital power"![6] It doesn't matter if your body is currently as dead as Sarah's once was. When God gives strength where you have no might, you are no longer dry and barren. You are fruitful and able to bear life! And when God heals your reproductive system, the rest of your body can operate at peak efficiency. When you secrete the right hormone levels, your metabolism runs like clockwork and your fat deposits shrink. Your muscles also get stronger, your body fights off disease, and your hair and skin become radiant!

This promise isn't only for the ladies. The word *virile* means "(of a man) full of strength, power, and energy in a way that is considered sexually attractive."[7] As men age, their testosterone levels drop dramatically, causing them to lose their energy, vigor, and sex drive. However, Isaiah 40 clearly states that God will turn that around and give them strength where they have no might.

So how does God fulfill these jaw-dropping promises? He does it through the righteous judgments He releases in His courts. Look at the verse that comes right before the passage of promises we are studying.

It asks, "Why do you say, O Jacob, and speak, O Israel: 'My way is hidden from the LORD, and my just *claim* is passed over by my God'?" (Isa. 40:27, NKJV). God's statement here includes a Hebrew word you've already seen: *mishpâṭ*, which is translated "claim" in this verse and means "a verdict" and "to plead any one's cause."[8]

Where are claims filed? In court! The Israelites were accusing God of passing over the just claim they had filed in His court. They wanted a verdict that His Word said was rightfully due them. But what kind of claim did they file? God's immediate response reveals what they were seeking: He said, "I give power to the weak and strength to those who have no might! You will run and not grow weary; you will walk and not grow faint!" (See Isaiah 40:29, 31, NKJV.) Their claim concerned their health, power over death, and ability to walk in youth restored!

The Israelites filed the same case that millions of believers petition for today. We want to be young, strong, and healthy again! No one wants to suffer chronic pain. People want to be free of disease and of reliance on medication. Believers hope to exercise without restrictions, to work and be productive, to enjoy life with their spouses and quality time with their children and grandchildren. People want to be healthy and live vibrant lives. Plus they want to love what they see when they look in the mirror.

God promises that all these things and more are possible when you file your just claim in His courts, then wait patiently for Him to fulfill His Word. Your ability to *patiently* wait on a righteous verdict from heaven's courts will determine whether your breakthrough comes.

Let Patience Have Its Perfect Work

The Bible tells us that patience can lead to a physical manifestation of youth restored. Let me prove it to you.

> But let patience have her perfect work, that ye may be perfect and entire, wanting nothing.
>
> —JAMES 1:4, KJV

The word translated "entire" here is the Greek *holoklēros*. *Thayer's Greek Lexicon* says it is used "of a body without blemish or defect"![9] God's thoughts are higher than ours. Somehow in His infinite wisdom He has ordained that building patience in us will, among other things, result in our bodies being healed and free of physical blemishes and defects, which often come with aging![10] This line of thought can be backed up by the fact that impatience, which is an opposing character trait, can breed stress, which according to doctors, will cause disease as well as premature aging. When we let patience have its perfect work, we not only grow spiritually but we also experience physical fruit in the form of youthful vitality.

Molting Like an Eagle

Once eagles acquire their fully matured plumage, they undergo an annual process of losing flight feathers and growing brand-new replacements. The process is called molting, and it continues through the eagle's lifetime. That is how God created this majestic bird to function. He enabled it to regenerate itself year after year so it could remain strong and healthy throughout its life span.

We were created to do the same. In our early years our bodies were capable of rapid cell turnover, which is why our skin and other organs always looked fresh and healthy. Unlike the eagle, however, our regeneration rate significantly slowed with age, leading to wrinkles and sagging skin, weight gain, and many other symptoms. Yet the Bible says we are supposed to be like eagles, continually regenerating even in our advanced years. So what's the deal?

As a forerunner in opening a new realm, I have experienced firsthand the tenacity, faith, and patience that it demands. As I pressed in for the revelation of youth renewal that few people walk in, the pain and price were high. Demonic resistance was massive, and the wait was excruciating. But when I chose to *patiently wait* while I continued to read, meditate on, and decree the instructions I found in Scripture, and as I included them in this study, I then began to see change in my physical body.

Waiting in Continual Expectation

God says that those who *wait* on Him will renew their strength and mount up, or soar, like eagles (Isa. 40:31). Does that mean you have to suffer in pain and desperation while you sweat it out and wonder whether God will show up?

Absolutely not! God is not a man that He should lie (Num. 23:19), and His Word never returns void to Him (Isa. 55:11). It's the *manner* in which you wait that determines your outcome. The following verse shows that those who *expectantly* wait for God to keep His promise will be changed and renewed, even while they look for their final manifestation!

> But those who wait for the Lord [who expect, look for, and hope in Him] *shall change* and renew their strength and power.
> —ISAIAH 40:31

This promise is fulfilled as you wait in an attitude of patience and expectation. Regeneration takes time. Before the eagle can grow new feathers, it has to lose the old ones; only then it sprouts new plumage. It's a process! The key is to maintain an attitude of patience and expectation, as these very characteristics will cause your growth to happen. Don't forget what James 1:4 says: "Let patience have her perfect work, that ye may be perfect and entire, wanting nothing" (KJV). Again, the word *entire* here is used "of a body without blemish or defect"![11]

The eagle accepts the process and doesn't get stressed out or offended while it waits to be regenerated, and its feathers are restored. In the same way your body will gradually be rebuilt and restored as you patiently and consistently study the biblical promises we are discussing.

I cite my own experience as an example of this. As the months and even years went by and I waited on the Lord, continuing to believe and decree the revelations in this book, my body slowly started transforming. My muscle mass steadily increased while my fat decreased. My muscles became more defined, and I got stronger even though I wasn't doing more exercise than normal. Overall I felt much better, and the chronic pain I had suffered my whole life began to diminish. My hair returned to its previous state of glory, and even my skin became clearer and tighter. At first it was hard for me to notice the shift because I saw myself every day. However, when I would run into people I hadn't seen for a while, they were always shocked at my appearance. Many said I looked much younger than I had when we first met many years prior.

Remember: "Faith comes by hearing, and hearing by the word of God" (Rom. 10:17, NKJV). Implanting the Word in your heart builds your faith. Then your hope and trust can grow, enabling you to wait with patience and expectation rather than vexation and doubt. This is what causes you to physically change and experience renewed strength and power. Faith is a substance that creates expectation, which in turn causes you to literally be renewed like the eagle. Your muscles steadily get stronger. Your skin becomes tighter, smoother, and brighter. Belly fat slowly decreases. Your pain lessens then totally leaves.

Am I saying you will never have a supernatural growth spurt? Not at all. I have seen thousands of miracles materialize in an instant! Even plants can surge overnight in size and fruitfulness when you fertilize them properly. That's why you need to reread every chapter in this book and keep decreeing the scriptures while you wait for, look for, and expect your miracle to show up!

Testimony

Since I began operating in the grace courts, I have seen many people with the most horrendous disorders receive justice. One is a woman named Jacqueline who received a miracle in our meeting in San Jose, California.

In February of the prior year, Jacqueline had an MRI. Immediately after the procedure she experienced a burning sensation that radiated down her left hip and into her thigh. She couldn't move, so her family rushed her to the hospital, where they shot her up with painkillers. After failing to find the cause of Jacqueline's suffering, doctors ordered a second MRI, after which Jacqueline's agony escalated. She felt like there was crushed glass in every joint of her body! If someone touched her hand or elbow, it caused terrible pain spasms. The same thing happened in her upper abdomen and feet. She described feeling as though something was constantly cutting her. Nothing seemed to help.

It was more than a year before Jacqueline discovered that she had gadolinium toxicity, an incurable condition caused by the metallic element (gadolinium) contained in the IV contrast administered during an MRI.[12] Gadolinium enables the imaging machine to "read" the patient's organs. The metal is supposed to leave the body through urination, but in many cases the patient's body holds on to it, with horrifying consequences.

Jacqueline and her husband arrived at our meeting late that night, so they sat way in the back. After a while I began praying for people who had metal in their bodies. I started by commanding their souls to be healed of the trauma. Then I asked the Holy Spirit and the angels to remove the metal from their systems.

Jacqueline came to the event with level-eight pain and very swollen ankles and legs. Less than a minute after I prayed, the swelling and pain disappeared completely! When she came forward to testify that she had been healed when I prayed, I hit her arms with a karate chop and raked my hands over her feet to test her healing. She had no pain whatsoever. Since then bloodwork for the presence of gadolinium has proved negative! As far as we know, Jacqueline is the only person to be healed of gadolinium poisoning. (You can watch her miracle testimony at the link provided in the notes.[13])

Entering the Grace Court

Let's talk about the protocol for entering the grace court. First and foremost, remember that it's all about Jesus. His sacrifice made it possible to win every case the enemy brings against you in court. And it is by grace through faith that you appropriate His saving work.

Always begin with worship and praise, because the Bible instructs you to "enter into His gates with thanksgiving, and…*His courts* with praise" (Ps. 100:4, NKJV). I always press into worship first, singing, dancing, praising, thanking the Lord, and praying in the Spirit.

Remember to come *boldly* to the throne of grace to obtain mercy and find grace in your time of need (Heb. 4:16). Be confident in Christ as you face your adversary, Satan, in court. Then prophetically decree Hebrews 4:16, which states your scriptural right to enter. Ask the Holy Spirit to accompany you as you approach the judge of all the earth. The Holy Spirit is your *Advocate* (John 14:26), "a person who pleads the cause of another in a court of law."[14] He is also your *Counselor*, meaning He's your "lawyer, especially a trial lawyer."[15]

Once in court, acknowledge the truth of the enemy's charges against you, and enter your guilty plea into the court record. A woman once chastised me severely for doing this, arguing that we should never agree with the enemy's accusations. All I can say is, she's probably never been cross-examined in a witness box! If you lie under oath, you'll be charged with perjury and sent to prison! I ought to know. When I was tried for my crimes, I lied my face off on the stand, then received a lengthy sentence.

As prosecutor, Satan wants to win his case, so he only uses viable evidence against you. Thus the charges against you are more than likely true. So when you go into court, do what Scripture tells you to do:

> Come to terms quickly [at the earliest opportunity] with your
> opponent at law while you are with him on the way [to court],
> so that your opponent does not hand you over to the judge,
> and the judge to the guard, and you are thrown into prison.
> —MATTHEW 5:25, AMP

People are scared of pleading guilty to charges brought against them. But remember that you are in the grace court, so there is more than enough grace present to wipe out your sins.

After you plead guilty, repent for all your lawbreaking and include the sins of your ancestors. Scripture says you overcome the enemy "by the blood of the Lamb and by the word of [your] testimony" (Rev. 12:11, NKJV). When you repent in heaven's courts, you testify of the blood's power to overcome every accusation!

Many people say that because you are under grace, you don't need to repent anymore. I disagree completely. Look at how these amazing verses connect repentance with the release of God's grace that has been freely given you:

> Blessed [forgiven, refreshed by God's grace] are those who mourn [over their sins and repent], for they will be comforted [when the burden of sin is lifted].
>
> —MATTHEW 5:4, AMP

> Blessed [forgiven, refreshed by God's grace] are you who weep now [over your sins and repent], for you will laugh [when the burden of sin is lifted].
>
> —LUKE 6:21, AMP

Repentance is how you enter into the grace that is already yours! Notice that these verses say you are refreshed by God's grace *when* you repent. I don't know about you, but I always feel reenergized after I take a shower and wash off all the dirt and sweat. That's what repentance does. It removes the grime of sin so that grace can invigorate, rejuvenate, and restore you.

Jesus said, "Repent, for the kingdom of heaven [including its courts] is at hand!" (Matt. 4:17, NKJV). He also instructed us to pray this every day: "And forgive us our debts [or trespasses], as we also have forgiven our debtors" (Matt. 6:12, NIV). Repentance is one of God's graces! It frees us and instantly negates our sin, which forces the enemy to back off!

I need to mention another important point here. There is such a thing as *overly* repenting. When you repent excessively, you step out of faith, not believing that your sins were totally forgiven through Christ's sacrifice. The Bible says Jesus died once for all so you could be made righteous. If you are constantly repenting and not moving into your victory, you probably don't believe that Jesus' sacrifice was enough.

Remember that you are saved by grace *through faith*. If you keep beating yourself up in repentance, you are not walking in faith. Therefore you will not access the grace you need to defeat the charges Satan has filed against you.

You must find balance. So how much repentance is enough? Look again at the marvelous verses in Matthew 5 and Luke 6. They show that God's grace refreshes those who repent, and they are comforted "when the burden of sin is lifted" (Matt. 5:4, AMP; Luke 6:21, AMP). That's your clue! When you feel the burden lift, you've hit the sweet spot! And please don't confuse Satan's condemnation with conviction from the Lord.

Personally I like to take Communion while I am in the court. It puts me and those before whom I testify in remembrance of what Jesus accomplished on the cross. (See Luke 22:19–20 and 1 Corinthians 11:24–25.) Partaking of the Lord's Supper pours His blood onto the sins being charged and wipes them out! It also heals your soul and body. (We will discuss the importance of this later.)

Also, when I am led by the Lord to do so, I enter the court with an offering. Psalm 96:8 says, "Give to the Lord the glory due His name; bring an *offering* and come [before Him] into His *courts*." Many of the accusations of sin against us are related to money. Whether you have sinned by overspending, being a careless steward, incurring debt, or failing to bring in all of your tithes, the enemy will file charges against you. For him it's another opportunity to release death in your body and even your finances.

I also ask the court to have Jesus testify on my behalf. Think about it: you are innocent because of Him! Hebrews 12:24 says He is the Mediator of the new covenant. This is His courtroom title. He mediates your covenant victory by testifying to (1) the total power of His cross to forgive your sin, and (2) the power of His grace to supersede the law you are charged with breaking.

Colossians 2 says the Lord's work on the cross undisputedly wipes out the charges against you, soundly defeating the enemy!

> [He] wiped out the handwriting of requirements that was against us, which was contrary to us. And He has taken it out of the way, having nailed it to the cross. Having disarmed

principalities and powers, He made a public spectacle of them, triumphing over them in it.

—COLOSSIANS 2:14–15, NKJV

This is such a powerful courtroom passage! The blood Jesus shed on Golgotha also can testify on your behalf. The verse that calls Jesus "the Mediator of the new covenant" also says that the sprinkled blood speaks of mercy (Heb. 12:24, NKJV). Yes, the blood has a voice! When Cain killed his brother Abel, I believe it was the spirit of death working through Cain to commit that murder. Genesis 4:10 says the Lord told Cain, "What have you done? The voice of your brother's blood is crying to me from the ground" (ESV). This indicates that Abel's blood testified against Cain and the spirit of death that drove Cain to murder! The blood of Jesus will do the same thing for you in court. Not only will the blood speak of its power to cleanse your sins so that a verdict of not guilty is rendered on your behalf, it will testify against death so your body can be healed.

Finally throw yourself on the mercy of the court so you can receive grace and mercy in your time of need. While in court, and even afterward, it is a must that you read, meditate on, and decree grace scriptures. They remind the enemy that you are under grace, and grace will always trump the law!

Grace Court Activation

Now it's time to enter the grace court. Listed below are some steps I mentioned earlier, followed by scriptures that you can declare while in court.

1. Begin by worshipping, singing, dancing, thanking our Lord, and praying in the Spirit before entering the court.

2. Next come boldly before the throne of grace, being confident in Christ. Say, "Lord, according to Your Word in Hebrews 4:16, I come boldly before the throne of grace to obtain mercy and find grace to help in my time of need."

3. As you stand before the judge of all the earth, say, "Holy Spirit, I ask You to come into court with me and be my representation. According to John 14:26 (AMP), You are my Advocate to plead my case, and You are my Counselor and trial lawyer."

4. Now enter a guilty plea with the court. Say, "Lord (or righteous judge), I enter a plea of guilty, acknowledging that the charges brought against me are true."

5. Next repent for sins that you and your ancestors have committed. Say, "As I take the witness stand, I repent for all my sins of lawbreaking. I do this on behalf of myself and my ancestors. I receive the gift of forgiveness that Jesus provided when He died on the cross of Calvary and took my sin upon Himself. I accept and receive His blood to cleanse me of every accusation, including those in my bloodline."

   (Take your time as you do this. Worship to a song about the blood and the power of the cross! Take Communion while worshipping, and decree that you are eating His body and drinking His blood in remembrance of what He accomplished on the cross for you. Stay in the place of repentance and worship until the burden of sin lifts and you are refreshed by God's grace.)

6. When you feel led, present an offering in the courts. If there are money-related sins in your life or bloodline, repent and ask the Holy Spirit where you should sow a seed.

7. Ask the court to have Jesus testify on your behalf. Say, "I humbly petition the court by asking that Jesus, the Mediator of the new covenant, would stand and testify on my behalf." (Worship while you wait for the Lord to testify.)

8. The blood of Jesus is alive and has a voice. Now say, "I ask the blood of Jesus that speaks a better message to speak on my behalf and testify to my innocence and against the spirit of death." (Worship while you wait for the blood to testify.)

9. Now say, "I throw myself upon the mercy of the court, and thank You that because of grace, Your mercy always triumphs over judgment."

Decrees Before the Court

Next decree the following scriptures. As you do, know that you are overcoming the enemy by the blood of the Lamb and your testimony on the witness stand.

Christ purchased our freedom [redeeming us] from the curse (doom) of the Law [and its condemnation] by [Himself] becoming a curse for us, for it is written [in the Scriptures], Cursed is everyone who hangs on a tree (is crucified).

—Galatians 3:13

For what the law could not do in that it was weak through the flesh, God did by sending His own Son in the likeness of sinful flesh, on account of sin: He condemned sin in the flesh, that the righteous requirement of the law might be fulfilled in us.

—Romans 8:3–4, nkjv

[He has] wiped out the handwriting of requirements that was against us, which was contrary to us. And He has taken it out of the way, having nailed it to the cross. Having disarmed principalities and powers, He made a public spectacle of them, triumphing over them in it.

—Colossians 2:14–15, nkjv

Personalize the following scriptures. Where the pronoun *you* or *your* appears, insert *I*, *me*, or *my*, as appropriate.

Sin shall not [any longer] exert dominion over you, since now you are not under Law [as slaves], but under grace [as subjects of God's favor and mercy].

—ROMANS 6:14

For it is by free grace (God's unmerited favor) that you are saved (delivered from judgment and made partakers of Christ's salvation) through [your] faith. And this [salvation] is not of yourselves [of your own doing, it came not through your own striving], but it is the gift of God.

—EPHESIANS 2:8

[All] are justified and made upright and in right standing with God, freely and gratuitously by His grace (His unmerited favor and mercy), through the redemption which is [provided] in Christ Jesus.

—ROMANS 3:24

But then Law came in, [only] to expand and increase the trespass [making it more apparent and exciting opposition]. But where sin increased and abounded, grace (God's unmerited favor) has surpassed it and increased the more and superabounded.

—ROMANS 5:20

Therefore, [inheriting] the promise is the outcome of faith and depends [entirely] on faith, in order that it might be given as an act of grace (unmerited favor), to make it stable and valid and guaranteed to all his descendants—not only to the devotees and adherents of the Law, but also to those who share the faith of Abraham, who is [thus] the father of us all.

—ROMANS 4:16

Now decree that death has no power over you. Then read the following verses aloud.

His own purpose and grace…has now been revealed by the appearing of our Savior Jesus Christ, who has abolished death and brought life and immortality to light through the gospel.

—2 TIMOTHY 1:9–10, NKJV

Since therefore the children share in flesh and blood, he himself likewise partook of the same things, that through death he might destroy the one who has the power of death, that is, the devil.

—HEBREWS 2:14, ESV

So that, [just] as sin has reigned in death, [so] grace (His unearned and undeserved favor) might reign also through righteousness (right standing with God) which issues in eternal life through Jesus Christ (the Messiah, the Anointed One) our Lord.

—ROMANS 5:21

Now decree the following youth-renewing verses (which are connected to the courts), along with the accompanying personal decrees.

Bless the LORD, O my soul; and all that is within me, bless His holy name! Bless the LORD, O my soul, and forget not all His benefits: who forgives all your iniquities, who heals all your diseases, who redeems your life from destruction, who crowns you with lovingkindness and tender mercies, who satisfies your mouth with good things, so that your youth is renewed like the eagle's. *The LORD executes righteousness and justice for all who are oppressed.*"

—PSALM 103: 1–6, NKJV

1. I decree that the Lord is pleading my case and executing His righteous verdict for me in the grace court! The death sentence inflicted by Satan for my lawbreaking is being overturned, and I am being issued what is lawfully due to me. I am forgiven of all my sins. My soul is blessed. All my

diseases are healed, and my youth is renewed like that of an eagle!

Then [God] is gracious to him and says, Deliver him from going down into the pit [of destruction]; I have found a ransom (a price of redemption, an atonement)! [Then the man's] flesh shall be restored; it becomes fresher and more tender than a child's; he returns to the days of his youth.

—Job 33:24–25

He shall pray to God, and He will delight in him, he shall see His face with joy, *for He restores to man His righteousness.*

—Job 33:26, NKJV

2. I decree that God has found an atoning sacrifice for me in His Son, Jesus Christ. By His grace I have been made righteous. Thus justice is being dispensed for me through the grace court. My skin is becoming fresher than a child's. My fat flesh and lean flesh are becoming like the days of my youth, and I am being revived from my sterility!

Why do you say, O Jacob, and speak, O Israel: "My way is hidden from the LORD, and my just claim is passed over by my God"? Have you not known? Have you not heard? The everlasting God, the LORD, The Creator of the ends of the earth, neither faints nor is weary. His understanding is unsearchable. He gives power to the weak, and to those who have no might He increases strength. Even the youths shall faint and be weary, and the young men shall utterly fall, but those who wait on the LORD shall renew their strength; they shall mount up with wings like eagles, they shall run and not be weary, they shall walk and not faint.

—Isaiah 40:27–31, NKJV

3. I decree that because of His grace, God has not passed over my just claim in court. He is pleading my case and will deliver a righteous verdict on my behalf! So as I wait patiently and expectantly on the Lord, He will renew my

strength. Step by step, He will give me might and virility!
He will cause strength to multiply and abound in my body.
I will not get discouraged during the molting process,
knowing that I will soon mount up with wings like eagles.
I will run and not be weary; I will walk and not faint. In
Jesus' name, amen.

Healing Commands

Now issue the following commands:

1. I command my soul to be healed of trauma, in Jesus'
   name.
2. I command all curses to break, in Jesus' name.
3. I command all spirits of infirmity to go, in Jesus' name.
4. I bind death's actions on my bodily organs, in Jesus' name.
   (List your organs and bind death off each one.)
5. I command all diseases, bacteria, and viruses to die, in
   Jesus' name.
6. I command all pain and its roots to be healed, in Jesus'
   name.
7. I ask for the Spirit of life to be released into every organ
   in my body and every part of my frame, from head to toe
   (including bones, blood, tissues, etc.), in Jesus' name.

Now, to see if your breakthrough has occurred, test yourself by doing
something you couldn't do before. Don't forget to share your testimony
with us by emailing it to me at selfies@katiesouza.com. (Be sure to hold
your phone in the landscape position.)

CHAPTER 6

TAKING YOUR BODY
AND SOUL TO COURT

M ANY YEARS AGO, well before I took on the spirit of death, God
told me I was going to become a "plain man," like Jacob.

Puzzled, I replied, "That doesn't sound very exciting, God,"
and immediately went to the Scriptures. I remembered that Jacob was
called "plain" in Genesis 25:27: "And the boys grew: and Esau was a cun-
ning hunter, a man of the field; and *Jacob was a plain man*, dwelling in
tents" (KJV).

My first impression was a sense of relief because I had always been horribly addicted to food, like Esau. (Hear more of my story in my resource
Soul Food.) However, I had already experienced victory in that area, so I
became confused. What did God mean by saying that I would be plain
like Jacob? To find out, I studied Genesis 25:27 and learned that the
Hebrew word for *plain* is *tam*, which can mean "complete, perfect...one
who lacks nothing in physical strength, beauty"![1]

Wow! Jacob was a hottie, and his life story proves it. Two women
fought fiercely for his love, even though it's estimated that he first married when he was eighty-four![2] Jacob eventually had twelve sons and a
daughter, which is a lot for an old guy. Being the grandchild of Abraham
and Sarah, he must have inherited their blessing of youth. So what
empowered him to possess what they had?

The answer is the courts. Read again what the Bible said about Jacob:
he "was a plain man, *dwelling in tents*" (Gen. 25:27, KJV). The Hebrew
word for *dwelling* is *yashab*, which can mean "to sit down (specifically as
judge)."[3] Did you catch that? I don't think Jacob hung out like a couch
potato in the tents while Esau went out and hunted for the people's food.

I believe the fact that Jacob dwelled in tents, unlike his brother, could mean he sat down as a judge, just settling disputes in the tents of his family and servants.

Breaking Down Traditions About Jacob

I need to break down some old mindsets about Jacob. We have been taught that he was a deceiver because he "tricked" his brother Esau out of the firstborn blessing. Actually that is not true. When Jacob and his mother, Rebekah, deceived Isaac, they acted to fulfill the word of the Lord concerning Jacob's life. That word came when he and Esau were in the womb together, struggling against each other. Rebekah asked the Lord what the conflict was about. He told her there were two nations in her womb, and the elder would "serve the younger" (Gen. 25:23, NKJV).

That means God Himself ordained Jacob and not Esau to receive the firstborn blessing! Further proof is found in Romans 9:13, where God said, "Jacob I have loved, but Esau I have hated" (Romans 9:13, NKJV).

Jacob's name means supplanter,[4] which is someone who "take[s] the place of (another), as through force"![5] Jacob was forcefully taking what was his! And when grabbing Esau's heel didn't work, Jacob and his mother took the steps they thought were necessary to ensure Jacob took the place ordained for him; thus they "tricked" Isaac into blessing Jacob.

Jacob as Judge

Knowing this makes it easier to understand why I believe the reference to Jacob dwelling in tents could mean he sat down as a judge. The firstborn spot belonged to him! He had a God-given calling to lead his people. This also explains how Jacob could be "complete, perfect...one who lacks nothing in physical strength, beauty."[6] As someone who recognized his responsibility to judge, Jacob would have understood that he also was competent to judge any issues within his own life or body that were contrary to the youth-restoring power his ancestors walked in.

The Bible says that your body is the "tent" you live in on earth (2 Cor. 5:1). Jacob was a plain man, dwelling among the tents. I believe Jacob understood his right to judge his physical tent whenever it fell into sickness or disease. That is why he lacked nothing in physical strength and beauty.

We Are All Judges

The New Testament says we are all judges who are granted permission to adjudicate every issue pertaining to our lives:

> Do you not know that the saints will judge the world? And if the world will be judged by you, are you unworthy to judge the smallest matters? Do you not know that we shall judge angels? How much more, things that pertain to this life?
> —1 CORINTHIANS 6:2–3, NKJV

That verse is loaded. God has called all believers to judge the world and even angels. That is high-level authority and carries with it a huge responsibility. We must not use this power to judge people. We are to use it to judge sin, injustice, and anything in ourselves that exalts itself against Christ as Lord and King. (See Matthew 7:1–5.) This includes bad behaviors and all kinds of diseases and disorders.

By His stripes Jesus has already won your total healing. That gives you the right to judge even the "smallest matters" and all "things that pertain to this life" (1 Cor. 6:2–3). If anything in your soul or body contradicts the victory for which Christ died, it is your duty to judge it so that Jesus can receive the just reward of His sacrifice!

Whatever you are facing that's not lined up with God's perfect will (as expressed in His Word) is fair game for you to judge. There might be issues in your marriage, problems with your children, failures in your business or ministry, cancer, heart disease, diabetes, blood disorders, pain, weakness, and illnesses of any kind. And because the Word gives you permission to judge even the smallest matters, why not add every menopausal symptom, metabolic failure, fat bulge, and skin problem? After all Jesus is purifying a bride "without spot or wrinkle" (Eph. 5:27).

The Scriptures show that Jesus judged a "fever" afflicting Peter's mother-in-law. The story is told in three different Gospels (Matt. 8:14–15; Mark 1:29–31; and Luke 4:38–41), so it must be hugely significant. Let's take a look at the story:

> He arose out of the synagogue, and entered into Simon's house. And Simon's wife's mother was taken with a great fever; and they besought him for her. And he stood over her, and rebuked the fever; and it left her: and immediately she arose and ministered unto them.
>
> —LUKE 4:38–39, KJV

I believe Peter's mother-in-law may have been suffering hot flashes rather than a fever. *Pyretós* (the Greek word translated "fever" in Luke 4:38) can be defined as "fiery heat," and "interpreters now give it the sense of 'fever.'"[7] All I can say is, those interpreters must have been men. It's very possible that Peter's mother-in-law was suffering the fiery heat of a hot flash! The disciples were said to be in their early to mid-twenties, which would put Peter's mother right around the age when women are in menopause.[8]

If you've ever had a hot flash, you know the magnitude of the heat it releases in the body. It's brutal and usually accompanies other equally dreadful symptoms. Both Matthew and Mark noted that Peter's mother was so stricken by this fiery heat that she was laid up in bed!

When I first read that, I thought, "It can't be a hot flash. No one is bedridden because of a hot flash." Now I say, "Oh really?"

I distinctly remember the morning I couldn't get out of bed because hot flashes kept me up the night before! The torment was intense. Wave after wave of great, fiery heat blazed across my body, causing me to sweat. Then, whenever that flash would let up, I turned freezing cold. One after the other the flashes came, forcing me to throw the blanket on and then off again. This continued all night long. By morning I was so exhausted I couldn't get out of bed.

No wonder Peter's mother-in-law was laid up!

So what did Jesus do about it? He rebuked the fever, and it left. The word for *rebuked* is *epitimáō* in the Greek, which means "to adjudge."[9]

This is courtroom terminology. *Merriam-Webster*'s definition of *adjudge* is "to decide or rule upon as a judge."[10] Jesus took that hot flash to court, where heaven ruled in the woman's favor! The fever left, and Peter's mother immediately arose and began serving!

It's so hard to serve God with your total energy, focus, and commitment when you don't feel well. Whether you have a deadly disease or are in menopause, the enemy will use it to keep you on the sidelines. However, when you drag your enemy and your symptoms into the grace court and judge them, you will receive a righteous verdict. Then you will be free to arise to serve the King—just as Peter's mother-in-law did!

Warning: I had to be just like the persistent widow to get the breakthrough over my unholy hot flashes. It was only after I took that fiery heat to the grace court many times and also partook of massive Communion (I will speak on that later in the book) that I finally conquered this extremely aggravating issue.

I can't resist adding something here. In the Book of Judges, God sent a judge named Ehud to deliver the Israelites from Eglon, the king of Moab. The Bible describes Eglon as "a very fat man" who oppressed Israel for eighteen years (Judg. 3:17). Interestingly enough the number eighteen is *shĕmoneh* in the Hebrew, which means "plumpness."[11]

Could the same evil spirit that empowered Moab's fat king to oppress Israel still be at work to afflict us with unpleasant plumpness today? I believe so! But what should we do about it? The answer is simple: go to court to judge that spirit and the fat it causes! That's what Ehud did. Don't forget, he was a judge sent by God to bring judgment on all the enemies of Israel. He took a long, double-edged sword and stabbed Eglon right where it counted—in his big, fat belly!

Take the sword (the Word that reveals these truths) into court, and judge every bulge that evil spirit has put on your lean and fat flesh. Then watch as you return to the days of your youth!

Perfect and Complete, Inside and Out

Jacob was not only perfect, complete, and full of physical strength and beauty, but his soul was also healed. The word translated "plain" in Genesis 25:27 also means to be "whole, upright, always in a moral sense."[12]

As I said earlier, Jacob was not the deceiver he's been cracked up to be. The Bible said he faithfully worked for his uncle, Laban, for twenty years, making Laban a very rich man. Jacob stayed even after Laban cheated him out of his wages and tricked him into marrying the wrong daughter. Jacob also remained married to Leah, though it was Rachel whom he really loved. That shows a lot of integrity and character on Jacob's part!

What empowered Jacob to act in such a moral and upright way despite his uncle's abusive treatment? I believe he consistently brought judgment against any attitude or behavioral problem that caused him to displease God.

This is what the Lord calls you and me to do—to judge any ugliness in our souls. Here's the proof:

> If we searchingly examined ourselves [detecting our short-comings and recognizing our own condition], we should not be judged and penalty decreed [by the divine judgment]. But when we [fall short and] are judged by the Lord, we are disciplined and chastened, so that we may not [finally] be condemned [to eternal punishment along] with the world.
>
> —1 CORINTHIANS 11:31–32

You are called to be the first to examine, detect, and recognize your own sins and shortcomings. As long as you do this, you won't face divine judgment in the courts. This is the way you beat Satan to the punch! Judge your attitude problems before he can, and he will have nothing left to bring accusations against you. This is how you stay ahead of the enemy and his endless attempts to put death on you.

Soul Healing and Defeating Death

As we've discussed, I believe Jacob was morally upright because he exercised his ability to judge himself. In addition he was perfect and complete, lacking nothing in physical strength and beauty. Did you know that moral uprightness is connected to physical strength and beauty? The more healed you are in your soul, the further you will go in climbing and defeating the mountain of aging, death, and disease. Look at what Scripture says about this:

> Beloved, I pray that you may prosper in every way and [that your body] may keep well, even as [I know] your soul keeps well and prospers.
>
> —3 JOHN 2

There is a direct connection between your soul's well-being and your physical health. One of the biggest ways to defeat death's effects on your body is to judge the behaviors that begin in your inner man. Then you will prosper in your health, even as your soul prospers!

The Wounded Soul

Your spirit was made perfect *instantly* upon your conversion. But your soul was not. Your mind, will, and emotions must undergo a continual healing process. In fact the Bible says your inner man can be wounded by traumatic events, sins you commit, and iniquities in your bloodline.

Isaiah 30:26 demonstrates how sin wounds the soul. It says, "The Lord binds up the hurt of His people, and heals their wound [inflicted by Him because of their sins]." That means sin can form wounds in your soul! The word translated "hurt" or "wound" is *sheber* in the Hebrew. It can mean "breach," or "fracture," and it includes the idea of "the mind being broken."[13] Any kind of sin can wound your mind and any part of your soul—including the sin of your own lawbreaking. Breaking the law not only gives Satan grounds to accuse you in court, but it also wounds your soul. Satan loves that because he is always looking for a "landing strip" to attack legally. The wounds in your soul give him that access.

Look at what Jesus said about this in John 14:30:

> I will not talk with you much more, for the prince (evil genius, ruler) of the world is coming. And he has no claim on Me. [He has nothing in common with Me; there is nothing in Me that belongs to him, and he has no power over Me.]

Here Jesus gives you a huge insider secret! The enemy gets his legal right to attack you when you share something in common with him. Those "in common" areas are the wounds in your soul that sin produced.

Remember that it's impossible to keep the whole law. Therefore every single Christian has been wounded by his or her own lawbreaking. Once this happens, those unhealed areas in your soul allow death to age you and deposit disease and disorder in your body. Take a look at this revealing verse, which clearly proves this point: "Now sin is the sting of death, and sin exercises its power [upon the soul] through [the abuse of] the Law" (1 Cor. 15:56).

Death can inflict its sting on your body because there are wounds in your soul that came from your lawbreaking. Are you exhibiting unhealthy behaviors such as unforgiveness, bitterness, offense, anger, and the like? If so, your soul is wounded and death is probably at work in your bodily organs. This is why getting your soul healed is so vitally important. It's the only way you can totally win the war against death!

But how do you do it? Through the power of grace! Grace not only wipes out all charges of lawbreaking but also heals your inner man. Let's take a closer look.

The Soul-Healing Power of Amazing Grace

When I minister, I often speak about *dunamis* power. Acts 1:8 says, "You shall receive power when the Holy Spirit has come upon you" (NKJV). The word translated "power" is *dynamis* (pronounced dü'-nä-mēs, as in *dunamis*). It means "excellence of soul."[14]

When you received Jesus as Lord, the Holy Spirt came to live in you. He didn't come alone however. He brought dunamis power with him. That means all believers have a tankful of dunamis that gives them the ability to heal every wound in their souls. I've seen thousands of miracles materialize when people become "excellent of soul" through the power of dunamis.

So imagine my delight when I discovered that grace is another potent soul-healing power freely available right when you need it. In fact dunamis is the power that *bestows* grace on you. Look at what Paul said about this in the Book of Ephesians:

> Of this [Gospel] I was made a minister according to the gift of God's free grace (undeserved favor) which was bestowed on me by the exercise (the working in all its effectiveness) of His power.
>
> —EPHESIANS 3:7

The Greek word for *power* in this verse is *dunamis*. This indicates that Paul received God's free gift of grace through the exercise of dunamis power. Dunamis confers God's grace on you! Whenever you release it, His grace flows wherever you need it, including into your soul to make it excellent.

Grace is often described as unearned, unmerited favor. However, it is much more than that! It is a soul-healing power. The Greek word translated "grace" is *charis*. One of its meanings is "the merciful kindness by which God, exerting his holy influence upon souls, turns them to Christ, keeps, strengthens, increases them in Christian faith, knowledge, affection, and kindles them to the exercise of the Christian virtues."[15]

Grace is a holy influence that turns your soul toward Christ, keeping and strengthening it and kindling your soul to exhibit godly virtues and behaviors. This means that grace can protect your soul when trauma assails it and reinforce it when you are emotionally and mentally weak, and even cause you to display Christ's qualities and characteristics—not because you are perfect but because grace kindles your soul to act right.

Grace, like dunamis, is a soul-healing power! Here's some biblical proof:

> The grace of God (His unmerited favor and blessing) has come forward (appeared) for the deliverance from sin and the eternal salvation for all mankind. It {grace} has trained us to reject and renounce all ungodliness (irreligion) and worldly (passionate) desires, to live discreet (temperate, self-controlled), upright, devout (spiritually whole) lives in this present world.
>
> —Titus 2:11–12

According to Paul's letter to Titus, grace not only delivers you from sin and gives you eternal life but also trains your soul to behave in a godly manner! When grace is working in your soul, you will be so changed that you won't want to engage in ungodly activities. You will easily reject worldly passions and be empowered by self-control to live a righteous life!

Grace is so powerful that it can strengthen you right in the middle of the worst adversities you have ever faced. Paul explained it to Timothy this way: "So you, my son, be strong (strengthened inwardly) in the grace (spiritual blessing) that is [to be found only] in Christ Jesus" (2 Tim. 2:1).

Grace is a spiritual blessing that can empower you to be "strengthened inwardly" in your mind, will, and emotions! It's interesting that right after Paul gave Timothy this good news, he warned him about the many hardships he would have to endure as a soldier of Christ (2 Tim. 2:3). I love that Paul forewarned Timothy of impending battles *after* letting him know that grace would be available to strengthen his soul in the middle of the struggle.

Have you ever faced a horrible situation that rocked you to your core? If so, you know how desperately your soul needed strengthening. Grace is a supernatural power that can support and fortify every part of your inner man, even when you feel like you can't handle one more thing. It's the free, unearned, and undeserved favor and mercy of God to heal your soul when you desperately need it.

Grace is even powerful enough to heal offenses, resentment, hatred, and any deep, bitter root in your soul. Look at this proof:

Exercise foresight and be on the watch to look [after one another], to see that no one falls back from and fails to secure God's grace (His unmerited favor and spiritual blessing), in order that no root of resentment (rancor, bitterness, or hatred) shoots forth and causes trouble and bitter torment, and the many become contaminated and defiled by it.

—HEBREWS 12:15

I love this verse for so many reasons. First of all, it admonishes me never to fall back from grace, because when grace is operating in my life, it can prevent bitter roots from growing in my soul.

When you let bitterness, resentment, rancor, or hatred gain a foothold in your life, trouble and torment follow. The root of the word *trouble* in Hebrews 12:15 is *ochleō* in the Greek. It means "to be vexed, molested, troubled: by demons."[16] Don't forget that a soul wound causes you to have something in common with the enemy. Your wounded soul gives Satan the legal right to vex, molest, and trouble you. But grace heals the roots of bitterness in your inner man and kicks the devil to the curb.

Deliverance Through Grace

I distinctly remember the first time my soul was healed by the power of grace and the deliverance that followed. For several weeks my husband and I had been bickering about stupid things. Finally, as we stood in the kitchen one day, he asked, "What is wrong with you?"

I stared at him defiantly and said, "I'm not the one who has the problem."

"Really?" he replied. "Lately you've become so selfish!"

I didn't respond. He had never called me selfish before. In fact a hallmark of our marriage was my constant care for him. I had always gone out of my way to see to his needs, so I thought for sure that he was wrong.

Later that day, I lay down for nap and listened to a CD I'd made with grace scriptures.[17] While praying along with the disc, I fell asleep and had an encounter. As the scriptures played, I felt the power of the Lord come upon me. Then I saw a vision of my heart, which was discolored and somewhat black. Suddenly it changed to a healthy-looking hue, just as I saw an evil spirit being taken out of it.

I woke up and asked God, "What was that?"

He answered, "A spirit of selfishness."

Unfortunately my hubby was right. I didn't tell him because I didn't want him to gloat. But in our kitchen a few weeks later he asked, "OK. What happened?"

At a loss to catch his meaning, I looked at him and asked, "What are you talking about?"

"Well," he replied, "you've changed in the last couple of weeks, so something went down."

Shrugging my shoulders, I smirked and continued cutting veggies. But I knew what he was talking about, and I never forgot it.

The Courts and Soul Healing

If you want to utterly conquer Satan, you must go to court, but you must also heal the legal ground in your soul that he's using to put sickness and death on you. Look at this powerful example of the woman who was bowed over with the spirit of infirmity:

> Now He was teaching in one of the synagogues on the Sabbath. And behold, there was a woman who had a spirit of infirmity eighteen years, and was bent over and could in no way raise herself up. But when Jesus saw her, He called her to Him and said to her, "Woman, you are loosed from your infirmity." And He laid His hands on her, and immediately she was made straight, and glorified God.
>
> —LUKE 13:10–13, NKJV

This woman had a spirit on her that was able to bend her spine! It kept her in that painful condition for eighteen years! When I first read the story, I asked the Lord what legal right the devil had to afflict her. His answers were contained in the language of this story. Let me share them with you now.

The Greek word translated "infirmity" is *asthéneia*, which means, "weakness, infirmity...of body...of soul"![18] This indicates the woman had something in her soul that was in common with that spirit of infirmity. That's why it had power to bend her bones. However, her wounded soul wasn't the only issue. As you will see, Satan had also filed a court case against her.

Jesus dealt swiftly with both issues. First He went to bat for her in court. Verse 12 says, "But when Jesus saw her, He called her to Him and said to her, 'Woman, you are *loosed* from your infirmity'" (NKJV). The Greek word for *loosed* is *apolyō*, which means "to acquit one accused of a crime and set him at liberty"![19] When Jesus "loosed" that woman, He took that spirit of infirmity to court and got the woman acquitted of the crime Satan had charged against her. Next Jesus healed the wound in her soul that she had in common with the spirit of infirmity. The Bible says, "He laid His hands on her, and immediately she was made straight, and glorified God" (v. 13, NKJV).

How did Jesus' laying His hands on her cause her soul to be healed? Acts 10:38 says, "God anointed Jesus of Nazareth with the Holy Spirit and with power, who went about doing good and healing all who were oppressed by the devil, for God was with Him" (NKJV). The word for *power* here is a Greek word we have seen before: it's *dynamis* (or *dunamis*)! Jesus was anointed with the excellence of soul power that dunamis releases. He used this restorative power to heal all who were oppressed by the devil, including the woman bent over by an evil spirit! When Jesus laid hands on her, He released dunamis power into her soul. Immediately she was healed of everything she had in common with that spirit and, after eighteen years, she stood up straight! That is God's amazing grace, imparted by dunamis power.

It's not enough to go into the courts and face the legal accusations against you. You must also get your soul healed of everything you have in common with the devil. The good news is that the grace court can accomplish both!

Testimony

While doing a meeting in Kansas, I taught on the grace court and the healing of the soul. On the second night I began to work miracles. That's when I met a woman named Lacie. Her spine was a mess. She had been in a violent car accident twenty years before, which caused the lower part of her spine to severely dip inwards as well as twist to the right. (This was confirmed by a nurse at the meeting named Pam, who checked Lacie's back before the prayer activation.) Lacie suffered massive pain from her injuries. At the meeting she could barely get in and out of her chair. In fact she was in so much pain that her family brought her wheelchair to the meeting just in case she could no longer walk. Her mother, Karen, came up to testify about Lacie's condition. Karen said Lacie was in such bad shape that she went over to Lacie's house every morning to help her with the kids, clean her house, and get her ready for the day.

After I lead the whole group into an activation in the court and positioned them to get their souls healed, I asked people to come up and testify. Lacie was one of them. She said the pain in her spine was gone and now she only felt muscle discomfort. So I invited the nurse, Pam, back up to examine her back. Upon touching Lacie, Pam immediately said, "You know, God is so awesome!...When you see these backs, you know they [the angels] have been busy!" Pam reported that Lacie's back was "good!" Then Lacie bent over and touched her toes with no pain at all! When I asked Karen if she had ever seen her daughter do that before, she said, "No! Not in a long time!"

Lacie then began to tell me how she had woken up that morning with level-nine pain and could barely move. That's when she went into the grace court, even though she had just learned about it the night before in my meeting. Even though she had never done it before, her pain immediately went from a nine to a five! She had been taking two oxycodone a day along with two Lyrica, but she didn't take any of her daily medications and then received her full healing that night. (You can watch Lacie's miracle testimony at the link in the notes.[20])

The Grace Court Does Double Duty

You can go boldly into the grace court not only to have charges of law-breaking dismissed against you but to get your soul healed at the same time. The Bible indicates that we can find justice for soul and body in the courts:

> My soul yearns, yes, even pines and is homesick for the courts of the Lord; my heart and my flesh cry out and sing for joy to the living God.
>
> —PSALM 84:2

David's heart and flesh—his body and soul—longed to go before the Lord because that is where he would find justice. The same is true for you.

As you stand in the witness box testifying about grace, its power will be present to get everything done! Now step back into the grace court and prepare to receive a whole new level of breakthrough. Before you go in, make a list of every issue in your body and soul that is not perfectly aligned with the Word of God and the victory Jesus won for you on the cross. You're going to take that list into court with you!

Activation of Grace for Body and Soul

Keep these things in mind as you prepare to enter the court:

1. As always, before entering the court, take time to worship, sing, dance, pray in the Spirit, and thank our Lord.

2. Now come boldly before the throne of grace, being confident in Christ. Prophetically step into the grace court by decreeing Hebrews 4:16 as your biblical right. Say, "Lord, according to Your Word in Hebrews 4:16, I now come boldly before the throne of grace to obtain mercy and find grace to help in my time of need."

3. Next announce your intent to file cases against every item on your list. Say, "Lord, my righteous judge, I humbly submit for the court's consideration motions of judgment against everything in my body and soul that does not line up with Your Word. I bring my case to court based on my biblical right to judge all matters that pertain to life, even the smallest matters. I do as Jesus did when He rebuked the fiery heat (fever) suffered by Peter's mother-in-law. Jesus took her affliction to court and judged it. I act as Ehud did when he judged the fat king Eglon, but I judge with the sword of the Word. I act like Jacob and sit as a judge among the tents so I can be morally upright, perfect, complete, and lacking nothing in physical strength and beauty. I am here to judge everything in me that doesn't align with everything Jesus won for me on the cross so that I may bring Him glory. I ask that cases be opened against the following grievances in my body and soul that are causing me extreme suffering and distress."

4. (Now read your list.)

Scriptures and Decrees

Now read aloud the following grace scriptures and the decrees that go with them. As you do, believe and decree that grace not only destroys the charges against you but also heals your soul of every wound that has given Satan and death the right to assault you. Where the Scripture uses pronouns like *you* or *ye*, personalize it with *me* or *I*.

> Laboring together [as God's fellow workers] with Him then, we beg of you not to receive the grace of God in vain [that merciful kindness by which God exerts His holy influence on souls and turns them to Christ, keeping and strengthening them—do not receive it to no purpose].
> —2 CORINTHIANS 6:1

I decree that grace is a holy influence that turns my soul toward Christ, keeps my soul, protects it, strengthens it, and heals it of any wounds the enemy is using as his legal ground to put death on me. Grace also kindles my soul to the exercise of Christian virtues. I decree that I have not received God's free grace in vain or without purpose. I will work its power, and because it can heal my soul, I will display the qualities and characteristics of Christ in every area of my thinking, choices, and emotions, in Jesus' name.

> For the grace of God (His unmerited favor and blessing) has come forward (appeared) for the deliverance from sin and the eternal salvation for all mankind. It {grace} has trained us to reject and renounce all ungodliness (irreligion) and worldly (passionate) desires, to live discreet (temperate, self-controlled), upright, devout (spiritually whole) lives in this present world.
>
> —Titus 2:11–12

I decree that grace is training my soul to act right! It is rebuilding my inner man so I won't even want to be involved in ungodly activities. By the power of grace, I renounce all worldly, passionate desires. Grace will empower me to have self-control and to live godly and upright in every area, in Jesus' name.

> So you, my son, be strong (strengthened inwardly) in the grace (spiritual blessing) that is [to be found only] in Christ Jesus.
>
> —2 Timothy 2:1

> You therefore must endure hardship as a good soldier of Jesus Christ.
>
> —2 Timothy 2:3, NKJV

I decree that grace is a spiritual blessing that strengthens me inwardly in my mind, will, and emotions. No matter what hardships, distresses, sorrows, griefs, sufferings, pains, agonies, persecutions, or trauma I endure as a good soldier in Christ, I can be strong because grace is working in me. Grace is the free, unearned, and undeserved favor and mercy of God, and it is available to heal me at any time, even amid major crises. I thank God for this amazing gift, in Jesus' name!

> I commend you to the Word of His grace.... It is able to build you up and to give you [your rightful] inheritance among all God's set-apart ones (those consecrated, purified, and transformed of soul).
>
> —ACTS 20:32

I decree that God's grace is building me up where I am weak. It is consecrating me and making me holy. God's grace is purifying and cleansing my soul. It is transforming my thinking by renewing my mind and altering my will so that I choose the things of the Spirit. Grace is changing my emotions so they are healthy and whole. Grace is my inheritance, and I now release it into my soul by the power of dunamis and the action of the Holy Spirit, in Jesus' name.

> Exercise foresight and be on the watch to look [after one another], to see that no one falls back from and fails to secure God's grace (His unmerited favor and spiritual blessing), in order that no root of resentment (rancor, bitterness, or hatred) shoots forth and causes trouble and bitter torment, and the many become contaminated and defiled by it.
>
> —HEBREWS 12:15

I decree that I will never fall back from or fail to secure God's grace. I secure it in order that every root of resentment, rancor, bitterness, or hatred in my soul that gives Satan the right to trouble, vex, and molest me will be healed, in Jesus' name.

> May grace (God's favor) and peace (which is perfect well-being, all necessary good, all spiritual prosperity, and freedom from fears and agitating passions and moral conflicts) be multiplied to you in [the full, personal, precise, and correct] knowledge of God and of Jesus our Lord.
>
> —2 PETER 1:2

I decree that through grace I have perfect well-being. Grace is healing my soul, so I am free from all fears, agitating passions, and moral conflicts. I believe that God's grace is being multiplied to me right now through the decreeing of His Word and the knowledge of God and Jesus, our Lord. I receive the increase of His grace now, in Jesus' name! Amen.

Now decree that death has no power over you, and say these verses aloud.

> His own purpose and grace... [have] now been revealed by the appearing of our Savior Jesus Christ, who has abolished death and brought life and immortality to light through the gospel {of grace}.
>
> —2 Timothy 1:9–10, NKJV

> [Just] as sin has reigned in death, [so] grace (His unearned and undeserved favor) might reign also through righteousness (right standing with God) which issues in eternal life through Jesus Christ (the Messiah, the Anointed One) our Lord.
>
> —Romans 5:21

Healing Commands

1. I command my soul to be healed of all wounds from sin and trauma, in Jesus' name.

2. I command all curses to break, in Jesus' name.

3. I bind death's actions on my bodily organs, in Jesus' name. (List your organs and bind death off each one.)

4. I command all spirits of infirmity to go, in Jesus' name.

5. I command all diseases, bacteria, and viruses to die, in Jesus' name.

6. I command all pain and its roots to be healed, in Jesus' name.

Now ask the Spirit of life to be released into every organ in your body and every part of your frame, from head to toe (including bones, blood, tissues, organs, etc.), in Jesus' name.

Now, to see if your breakthrough has occurred, test yourself by doing something you couldn't do before. Don't forget to share your testimony with us by emailing it to me at selfies@katiesouza.com. (Be sure to hold your phone in the landscape position.)

CHAPTER 7
THE LIGHT BRINGS LIFE

SOMETIMES PEOPLE TAP into grace then erroneously think they don't need to do anything but sit back and relax. Yet Jesus told us to pray, fast, preach the gospel, take the kingdom of heaven by force, take up serpents, drive out demons, heal the sick, cleanse lepers, raise the dead, and oh, so much more. (See Luke 11:1–4; Matthew 6:16–18; Mark 16:15; Matthew 11:12; Mark 16:18; and Matthew 10:8.)

Walking in grace doesn't excuse you from doing other good works. James 2:17 says, "Even so faith, if it hath not works, is dead, being alone" (KJV). The word translated "dead" is *nekros*, which means "a corpse"![1] You are fighting the spirit of death. If your faith is not accompanied by good works, your body will remain lifeless.

I love the wording of James 2:17 in the Amplified Bible, Classic Edition: "So also faith, if it does not have works (deeds and actions of obedience to back it up), by itself is destitute of power (inoperative, dead)." Grace is accessed by faith in Christ alone, but if your faith stays alone, without accompanying works, it will become emptied of power and produce nothing but a dead corpse!

You can't work for salvation. It is by free grace, through a gift of faith, that you are saved. However, once that happens, good works should naturally spring from your redemption.

Paul touched on the balance of grace that all believers should walk in:

> By the grace (the unmerited favor and blessing) of God I am what I am, and His grace toward me was not [found to be] for nothing (fruitless and without effect). In fact, I worked harder than all of them [the apostles], though it was not really I, but

the grace (the unmerited favor and blessing) of God which
was with me.

—1 CORINTHIANS 15:10

Paul worked harder than anyone to spread the gospel. Yet he knew he
had not done it through his own ability or righteousness. He credited his
good works to God's grace, and he echoed this sentiment in Philippians:

Therefore, my beloved, as you have always obeyed, not as in
my presence only, but now much more in my absence, work
out your own salvation with fear and trembling; for it is God
who works in you both to will and to do for His good pleasure.

—PHILIPPIANS 2:12–13, NKJV

You are called to work out your salvation but not in your own strength!
Paul says it will be God who works in you to do His perfect will.

His Light Brings Life

Once you stop the decay of death in your bodily organs, you need to
release into your body the power to be regenerated, rebuilt, and revived!
For the rest of this study we will look at the freely given supernatural
gifts that you need to operate in so that newness of life can saturate every
part of your being.

The first one is the light of Jesus Christ. As I unpack this truth, let me
make one thing clear: this is not witchcraft or New Age teaching. The
Bible says, "God is Light, and there is no darkness in Him at all" (1 John
1:5). The first thing God created in Genesis chapter 1 was light (verse 3),
because that is who He is. Consequently, when He spoke, what came out
of Him was His very essence in the form of light.

Jesus said, "I am the Light of the world" (John 8:12). The first chapter
of Hebrews goes into even more detail concerning this characteristic of
God and Christ. It says, "He is the sole expression of the glory of God
[the Light-being, the out-raying or radiance of the divine], and He is the
perfect imprint and very image of [God's] nature" (Heb. 1:3).

Jesus is the *Light-being*, the perfect imprint and image of God. Once

Jesus comes to live in you, He begins imprinting God's nature on you. He accomplishes this through the "out-raying" of His Light (mentioned in Hebrews 1:3). Just as light transfers an image from a photographic negative onto photo paper, the light coming from Jesus causes God's nature to be transmitted and developed in your soul and body. This is one of the ways you become conformed to the very image of Christ (Rom. 8:29).

This action is executed through the Holy Spirit, whom the Bible says is also Light. Look at this revealing verse in Ephesians 5:9: "The fruit (the effect, the product) of the Light or the Spirit [consists] in every form of kindly goodness, uprightness of heart, and trueness of life." Now let's break down the verse. The word Light is capitalized because the Bible is talking about Jesus, who is the Light of the world. Then the verse directly connects the Light to the Spirit, as though they are interchangeable, which they are. The Holy Spirit is the Spirit of Christ, living in you (Rom. 8:9).

Because Jesus is the Light of the world, the Spirit is also Light, and according to Ephesians 5:9, the Light produces fruit in your life. As the Spirit out-rays Christ's light from your spirit man into your soul and body, you become the image of Christ and are able to walk "in every form of kindly goodness, uprightness of heart, and trueness of life" (Eph. 5:9).

The Light produces the fruit of kindness, goodness, and uprightness in your soul and releases life-giving power into your body. Christ's light can heal every part of your being. It drives out the darkness of bad thinking, wrong motives, and dark, painful emotions. It also brings life to your organs and the parts of your body that are aging and decaying because of death.

The Soul-Healing Power of His Light

The healing of your inner man is of the utmost importance if you are to prosper in your health, even as your soul prospers. So let's look at the power of His light to heal your soul wounds, starting with this amazing scripture:

> Moreover, the light of the moon will be like the light of
> the sun, and the light of the sun will be sevenfold, like the
> light of seven days [concentrated in one], in the day that the
> Lord binds up the hurt of His people, and heals their wound
> [inflicted by Him because of their sins].
>
> —ISAIAH 30:26

Here the Lord promises a *massive increase* of His light on the earth—the light of seven days concentrated into one! Why would He do that? This verse says He does it to bind up the hurts of His people and heal the wounds inflicted because of their sin. This world is full of sin, thus billions of people are wounded and in desperate need of healing! God clearly states that He will meet their need and heal them through the intensifying of His magnificent light in their souls.

I cling to this prophecy because the church is full of pain and God's people need the light of Christ to invade their souls. The Bible says, "The heart is deceitful above all things…! Who can know it…?" (Jer. 17:9). This proves that our souls are a mess, full of manipulation and evil. But the Light can expose every dark deception that holds our souls captive. Look at what the psalmist wrote:

> Our iniquities, our secret heart and its sins [which we would
> so like to conceal even from ourselves], You have set in the
> [revealing] light of Your countenance.
>
> —PSALM 90:8

Light can pierce any darkness. It has been said that on a dark night (and if the earth were flat), you could see a candle flickering up to thirty miles away and perceive bright lights from hundreds of miles away![2] Now imagine how much brighter the light coming from Jesus is. His entire being is full of light. As you sit in the presence of His countenance through prayer and worship, His light penetrates your soul and reveals the secret sins that have been concealed from your understanding. That's when you are changed!

The light of Christ not only exposes the darkness and hidden motives in your soul but also heals them. Look at the evidence in Malachi 4:

> Unto you who revere and worshipfully fear My name shall the Sun of Righteousness arise with healing in His wings and His beams, and you shall go forth and gambol like calves [released] from the stall and leap for joy.
>
> —MALACHI 4:2

The word *beams* here refers to "a ray or shaft of light."[3] So Jesus Christ, the sun of righteousness, uses His beams to release healing in you. The word translated "arise" in Malachi 4:2 is *zarach*, which means "to irradiate (or shoot forth beams), i.e. to rise (as the sun)."[4] The word translated "healing" in the verse is *marpe'* in the Greek; it means "refreshing" and "tranquility of the mind."[5]

Your mind, which is part of your soul, desperately needs to be healed and renewed. The mind is the battlefield, as Joyce Meyer so aptly said.[6] We war against the thoughts that besiege us minute by minute. (That is a frightening thought!) The Bible says that as a person "thinks in his heart, so is he" (Prov. 23:7, NKJV). Consequently, if you dwell on the idea of divorcing your spouse, you will be divorced. If you continually think about how broke you are, you will remain in lack. If you repeatedly think about an offense that wounded you, it will become impossible to forgive the offender. If you meditate too long on quitting the ministry, you will quit. And if you allow yourself to believe that you're going to die from an illness, death will have its way.

Unless your mind is renewed, you will never conquer the mountain of death in order to possess life. The strongholds in your mind, including the dark thoughts implanted by the enemy, will rule you. But when the sun of righteousness arises on you, He transmits His character and His righteousness to you through His beams of light. Then your mind will become *marpe'*: refreshed and in a tranquil state. You will think righteous thoughts, and the enemy will have no ground from which to accuse you! Death's assignment will be broken, and you will do as Malachi prophesied: you will "go forth and gambol like calves [released] from the stall and leap for joy" (Mal. 4:2).

Luke's Gospel reiterates the theme of the soul being healed in His light. Take a look at this:

> Your eye is the lamp of your body; when your eye (your conscience) is sound and fulfilling its office, your whole body is full of light; but when it is not sound and is not fulfilling its office, your body is full of darkness. Be careful, therefore, that the light that is in you is not darkness. If then your entire body is illuminated, having no part dark, it will be wholly bright [with light], as when a lamp with its bright rays gives you light.
>
> — LUKE 11:34–36

Believe it or not, this is about healing your inner man. The eye is the window to the soul. Here Jesus reveals how each part of your soul can become "sound and fulfilling its office." But what does that mean? It's simple: your mind, will, and emotions were created by God to hold particular offices in your inner man and perform specific duties.

Among other things your mind was designed to rightly divide good thoughts from bad, form healthy powers of reasoning, and operate with a clean, creative imagination. So how do you heal the mind and free it to precisely execute its office? Jesus says it happens when "your whole body is full of light." His light drives out the darkness caused by wounds in your inner man. Those wounds control your thoughts, but when He heals them with His light, your mind becomes sound.

The job of your will is to make good Spirit-led decisions so you are not directed or controlled by the pain of your wounds. When your whole body is full of light, you become healed and able to discern "the perfect will of God" (Rom. 12:2). This empowers you to make good choices that lead to explosive prosperity instead of failure.

The light of Christ can heal every part of your inner man. Your emotions are no exception. When your whole body is full of light, your emotions become sound and able to fulfill their office too. Subsequently your reactions to the most trying and difficult circumstances will be healthy. Plus you will be filled with God-given passions instead of worldly lusts. And you will experience joy like never before because of the soul-healing power of His light!

The Light Is Medicine for Your Physical Body

The light of Christ not only heals your wounded soul but also your body. When Christ out-rays His light into your physical being, it acts like medicine with power to cure any disease. Let's look at Malachi 4:2 again:

> Unto you who revere and worshipfully fear My name shall the Sun of Righteousness arise with healing in His wings and His beams, and you shall go forth and gambol like calves [released] from the stall and leap for joy.

Christ arises on you with *healing* in the beams of His light. The word translated "healing" is *marpe'*, which also means "a cure," "literally (concretely) a medicine."[7] Thus His light can be the antidote for any disease, especially when you take it regularly, like medicine.

We know a wonderful couple in Europe, Angy and Luc, who are partners with this ministry. When they first heard my message on demonic kings and the healing power of Christ's light, they began to decree verses about light over their son, who was born autistic. The boy was three years old at the time and had never uttered a word or made a sound. He spent hours opening and shutting doors and cabinets. He never smiled or looked anyone in the eye. He also wouldn't let anyone hug or kiss him, which devastated his adoring parents.

Believing this was a spiritual issue, Angy cried out to the Lord, begging Him to lead her to someone who could help. Immediately the Holy Spirit instructed her to call a ministry in the United States at exactly 2:00 a.m. her time in the Netherlands. Thinking she was hearing nonsense, she asked the Lord to wake her up at that time if it was truly Him speaking. She awoke right before 2:00 a.m., so she made the call. The woman who answered said she felt it was a divine appointment that they were speaking because no one was ever in the office at that time. Then she promptly told Angy, "You need to get in touch with Katie Souza." She even provided Angy with our phone number.

Long story short, Angy contacted us, and we sent her some teaching resources, including a teaching on the light of Christ. Immediately Angy began to bombard their son with scriptures about the Light numerous times each day, dispensing the Word like medicine. She did this for six months with no change whatsoever! Then suddenly one day, while the therapist was present, a single, loud cry came pouring out of her child. From that moment on, his healing manifested. Then one day he approached his grandmother, took her face in his hands, looked her right in the eye, stroked her face, and then rubbed his nose back and forth on hers while kissing her. As the days passed, he smiled and even laughed. Next, the repetitive actions of opening and closing doors ceased, and he was on his way to becoming a whole new person!

Today, the boy speaks three languages, goes to school, rides horses, and is living the life of a happy, healthy kid. He was healed in both soul and body by the Light of the world, Jesus Christ. (You can watch their powerful testimony at the link provided in the notes.[8])

His Light Conquers Death and Releases Life

The Lord's light contains both power over death and pure vibrant life for your body. Look at this astounding proof: "You have delivered my life from death, yes, and my feet from falling, that I may walk before God in the light of life and of the living" (Ps. 56:13).

Both your deliverance over death and the power of life are found in His light. The Bible is replete with promises that Jesus can revive someone from death through the blazing light that emanates from Him. Here is another example:

> Because of and through the heart of tender mercy and loving-kindness of our God, a Light from on high will dawn upon us and visit [us] to shine upon and give light to those who sit in

darkness and in the shadow of death, to direct and guide our
feet in a straight line into the way of peace.

—LUKE 1:78–79

The Light that came down from heaven is Jesus, the Light of the
world. He appeared in part to give His healing light to those who are at
death's door, both spiritually and physically. When His light shines upon
them, they can emerge from death's deadly shadow and live.

In Him you "live and move and have [your] being" (Acts 17:28). In
the Book of John, Jesus comforts and encourages those who need life-
giving power by telling them it is contained in His light.

> He said, "I am the Light of the world. He who follows Me
> will not be walking in the dark, but will have the Light which
> is Life."
>
> —JOHN 8:12

We all have darkness within us, whether it is the gloom of wrong
thinking and wounded emotions or the shadow of sickness and death on
our physical bodies. Yet Jesus said that when we follow Him, we never
have to walk in darkness again. Instead we can have His light, which
brings life. The word *life* means "vitality, vigor, or energy."[9] His light is a
life-giving force that can heal our souls and flood our bodies with good
health, energy, youth, and robust stamina.

The word *life* also means "the capacity for growth, reproduction...and
continual change."[10] The light of Christ will cause new healthy cells to
develop and reproduce in your body, thus forming new skin, bone, tissue,
and brain matter. His light prompts the body to constantly renew itself
so that your body can run at maximum efficiency and look good while
doing it.

Did you know that light is involved in a huge percentage of cosmetic
treatments offered by practitioners in the esthetics industry? Light therapy
and laser devices harness and release light energy that triggers your body
to accelerate its natural skin renewal. It is a scientific fact that your "skin
uses light as a source of energy, to fuel the repair and rejuvenation of

damaged cells....The energy then stimulates the production of collagen and elastin, boosts circulation and accelerates tissue repair."[11] Doctors and cosmetologists recommend light therapy to treat "sun damage, acne, rosacea, eczema, psoriasis, dermatitis, sensitive and inflammatory conditions, wound healing and scarring."[12] It is also used to resurface and plump the skin, restoring its radiance and reducing wrinkles, spots, and sagging. When it comes to youth-renewing capabilities, light therapy has produced amazing results. Imagine, then, the power of God's light to transform your appearance!

Look at what happened when Jesus went up on the Mount of Transfiguration and was enveloped in God's light:

> And six days after this, Jesus took with Him Peter and James and John his brother, and led them up on a high mountain by themselves. *And His appearance underwent a change in their presence; and His face shone clear and bright like the sun,* and His clothing became as white as light....*While he was still speaking, behold, a shining cloud [composed of light] overshadowed them,* and a voice from the cloud said, This is My Son, My Beloved, with Whom I am [and have always been] delighted. Listen to Him!
>
> —MATTHEW 17:1–2, 5

Wow! When Jesus went up on that mountain, His appearance was changed, His face shone clear and bright, and a shining cloud of light overshadowed Him! Countless spas offer light therapy services that promise to change your skin's appearance by repairing and rejuvenating cells and making your skin clear and bright. But why spend thousands of dollars when you can tap into the light of Christ and the Spirit, which freely flows like rivers of living water from your innermost being? (See John 7:38.)

That is why Psalm 36:9 says, "For with You is the fountain of life; in Your light do we see light." A fountain of life is always available from within your spirit man. As you proclaim these truths over yourself, the light of the Holy Spirit responds by bringing life-giving power to every cell in your body.

I was in Jacksonville, Florida, teaching on the light of Christ when I received a word of knowledge that someone was being healed of flesh-eating bacteria. A woman came up and testified that she had been battling a fierce staph infection for years. Not only had it eaten a two-inch-deep hole in her armpit, but it also caused sores, swelling, and deafness in her right ear. The woman said her doctors had tried every type of antibiotic, to no avail. Yet when the life-giving fountain of Christ's light filled her, she said she was instantly healed. She said that not only did her deaf ear open and the sores and swelling disappear, but the hole in her armpit filled in! The bacteria that had eaten her flesh were destroyed, and her skin was completely rejuvenated and repaired in His light!

Don't forget, the same Spirit that raised Christ from *death* dwells in you and quickens your mortal body! (See Romans 8:11, KJV.) If the Holy Spirit, who is Light, could completely renew and rejuvenate Christ's physical body after He was horribly beaten and left dead in a tomb for three days, He can do the same for you.

His Light Heals the Worst Cases

One of the reasons Christ's light is such an effective weapon against sickness, unhealthy aging, and death is its power to penetrate the deepest, darkest places in your body and destroy any hidden disease. Think about it: X-rays are a form of light waves. They infiltrate the body and enable doctors to see into the bones and even the marrow to detect and treat injuries and illnesses.

Christ's light can penetrate and heal the most difficult diseases on earth. Look at the example of the boy who was epileptic and afflicted by a deaf and dumb spirit (Matt. 17:15; Mark 9:17–18, 25; Luke 9:39). A demon tried to kill the child many times, throwing him into fire to burn him and into water to drown him (Matt. 17:15). Much to his father's discouragement, no one could heal the poor boy—not even the disciples who, at that time, were the most skilled people on earth in healing and deliverance (Mark 9:18).

The good news is that Jesus quickly dispelled that demon and made the child whole again—and He did it through the power of His light. Jesus had just descended from the Mount of Transfiguration, where He had a supernatural encounter with God's presence and His clothing became as bright as light. The next day, Jesus met up with the afflicted child and the people who were trying to deliver him. The Bible says, "Immediately all the crowd, when they saw Jesus [returning from the holy mount, His face and person yet glistening], they were greatly amazed and ran up to Him [and] greeted Him" (Mark 9:15).

It's no coincidence how Scripture mentions that Jesus was still covered with light when He cured a child no one else could help! The sun of righteousness arose on that boy, with healing in His wings and beams!

Just like that child was freed of a deaf spirit, I see many ears healed when I teach on the light. I was in Minnesota when a man named Paul shared that for most of his life he heard the sound of doors slamming in his ears whenever he inhaled. Instantly all sound would become muffled, as though he were submerged in a bucket of water. Then, as he exhaled, the "doors" would open, and he would hear static and crackling sounds. When this occurred, he had to intently focus on whomever was speaking and what that person was saying. This unending process tormented and completely exhausted him.

That night, as I taught about the healing power of the Light, Paul received a miracle. As he stood on the stage demonstrating his healing, his eyes filled up with tears and he said (in shock), "It's not there. It's gone!" (You can watch Paul's healing testimony at the link provided in the notes.[13])

Your Voice Releases Light

When a car runs out of gas, it stops dead in the street. It's vitally important that you regularly fill up with "light fuel." So how do you release

His light from your spirit man into the rest of your being so you can bring life into every dark place?

It happens through your decrees.

The word translated "voice" in Mark chapter 1 is the Greek word *phōnē*.[14] The etymology of this word is likely related to the Greek word *phainō*, which means "to bring forth into the light, cause to shine, shed light to shine...be bright or resplendent, to become evident, to be brought forth into the light."[15]

Remember, the Holy Spirit is Light (Eph. 5:9). Your voice releases the light that's in your spirit to facilitate healing wherever you need it. Psalm 119:130 says that the entrance of God's words gives light! When you speak scriptures about the light of Christ, His light shines out of you, bringing everything into the light, where it becomes bright and resplendent!

When you decree scriptures about Christ's light, your voice releases its healing power. Look at this proof, from Job 22:28: "Thou shalt also decree a thing, and it shall be established unto thee: and the light shall shine upon thy ways" (KJV). I hear lots of people quoting the first half of that verse, but they leave out the best part. Your decrees are established because your voice releases His light into the gloom of sickness, death, and poverty, driving out everything that blocks your victory. Your decrees are established because His light shines upon your ways as you speak His Word!

That's why it is so crucial to watch what you say. When you talk badly about someone or complain about situations instead of being thankful, your voice releases the darkness in your soul rather than the light of Christ from your spirit. Scripture says, "Death and life are in the power of the tongue" (Prov. 18:21)! Negative words release death, but positive confessions of His Word release His light, which is life!

The Bible says even your praise releases His light!

> Praise the Lord! (Hallelujah!) I will praise and give thanks to the Lord with my whole heart in the council of the upright and in the congregation.
>
> —PSALM 111:1

117

The word *praise* is *halal* in the Hebrew, which means, "to shine…[to] give (light)…to make bright or shining."[16] When you praise the Lord, you release light from your spirit into every place you need it. I've seen people—countless people!—receive miracles just by praising Him. Although many people understand the power of praise, they don't always realize that their praise releases His healing light that positions them for victory.

Many Christians fall into the bad habit of complaining while they wait for their breakthroughs. This releases darkness and death into your situation and causes your miracle to be delayed even more. That's why 1 Thessalonians 5:18 says to give thanks in all things, "for this is the will of God in Christ Jesus concerning you" (KJV).

It's God's will that you give thanks in everything. Doing so releases light into whatever ails you and resolves it! In the midst of a crisis you need to break out in praise and thanksgiving, *no matter how you feel.* Then your praises will release the light of Christ that's in you so it can establish healing, breakthrough, and deliverance in the stubborn areas you face.

Even your hands carry and release light. The Bible is very clear about the doctrine of the laying on of hands (Luke 4:40; Acts 28:8). Scripture says God "covers His hands with the lightning and commands it to strike the mark" (Job 36:32). You're created in God's image; therefore you can lay hands on any part of your body (or on someone else) and command God's lightning to strike and heal any issues in the soul or disorders in the body!

Continue in His Light

In John 12, Jesus admonished all believers to continue relying on His light to solve their problems. He said, "While you have the Light, believe in the Light [have faith in it, hold to it, rely on it], that you may become sons of the Light and be filled with Light" (John 12:36).

Because the word Light is capitalized in this verse, we know Jesus is referring to Himself. But why didn't He just say, "Believe in Me"?

Why did He say, "Believe in the Light"? It's because He wants you to trust in this particular part of His character and nature. His light is extremely powerful and versatile. It can seek out and cure any problem. That's why Jesus said to "believe in the Light."

The Lord is admonishing you to believe that His light can do everything the Bible claims it can. He wants you to *rely* on it every time your soul needs help and your body is sick. He is warning you to *hold on* to the light by never letting this revelation fall by the wayside. If you keep receiving His light, you will become "sons of the Light" and "be filled with Light" (John 12:36).

Luke 11:36 says, "If then your entire body is illuminated, having no part dark, it will be wholly bright [with light], as when a lamp with its bright rays gives you light." As you get saturated with His light, it will shine from you like a lamp onto other people, and they will be healed too. That is one way you can operate in the miraculous!

Light Activation

As you decree the verses below, your voice will release the Light that is in your spirit man into every place you need it. Don't forget that when you decree something, it is established because the Light shines upon your ways. While making your decrees, make sure to lay your hands on any area where you need help so the lightning can strike its mark. (I also highly encourage you to get my teaching resource and companion soaking CDs *Sons of the Light*.)

> Moreover, the light of the moon will be like the light of the sun, and the light of the sun will be sevenfold, like the light of seven days [concentrated in one], in the day that the Lord binds up the hurt of His people, and heals their wound [inflicted by Him because of their sins].
>
> —Isaiah 30:26

Lord, I ask for this prophetic word to manifest now in its fullness on the earth and in my life so believers everywhere can access the multiplied intensity of your healing light. Lord, make one day of light equal to seven so we can be healed quickly of every wound that has resulted from our sin.

> Unto you who revere and worshipfully fear My name shall the Sun of Righteousness arise with healing in His wings and His beams, and you shall go forth and gambol like calves [released] from the stall and leap for joy.
>
> —MALACHI 4:2

I decree that the sun of righteousness, Jesus Christ, is arising on me with healing in His beams of light. His light is transmitting His righteousness into my soul so I will think and act in ways pleasing to God, as the light heals every wound in my inner man. I decree that I am receiving what *healing* (*marpe'*) means: refreshing and tranquility of the mind because of Christ's light.

> Your eye is the lamp of your body; when your eye (your conscience) is sound and fulfilling its office, your whole body is full of light; but when it is not sound and is not fulfilling its office, your body is full of darkness. Be careful, therefore, that the light that is in you is not darkness. If then your entire body is illuminated, having no part dark, it will be wholly bright [with light], as when a lamp with its bright rays gives you light.
>
> —LUKE 11:34–36

I decree that every part of my soul is becoming sound and fulfilling its office, in His light. My mind will think and reason rightly; I will have a clean, creative imagination, and I will possess a healed memory bank because my whole body is full of light.

I decree that my will is sound and fulfilling its office because Jesus is arising on me with healing in His light. My will is not controlled by the wounds in my soul because they are healed in His light. Instead my will now makes sound, Spirit-led decisions because my whole body is full of

His light. And because my will is healed, I make decisions that lead to extraordinary prosperity in my life.

I decree that my emotions are sound and fulfilling their office too. Thus I will have healthy reactions to every difficult circumstance, and I will walk in joy and peace no matter what I face. It's all because my whole body is filled with His light.

> The fruit (the effect, the product) of the Light or the Spirit [consists] in every form of kindly goodness, uprightness of heart, and trueness of life.
>
> —EPHESIANS 5:9

I decree that the Holy Spirit, who is Light, is releasing the light of Christ into my soul and body, and this will produce fruit in me. I decree that the effect and product of His light will be kindly goodness, uprightness of heart, and trueness of life. I will manifest the fruit of being kind, gentle, loving, righteous, moral, blameless, and upright in my soul, and I will experience the trueness of life in every place I desire it, including my physical body.

> He [Jesus] said, I am the Light of the world. He who follows Me will not be walking in the dark, but will have the Light which is Life.
>
> —JOHN 8:12

> You have delivered my life from death, yes, and my feet from falling, that I may walk before God in the light of life and of the living.
>
> —PSALM 56:13

> Because of and through the heart of tender mercy and loving-kindness of our God, a Light from on high will dawn upon us and visit [us] to shine upon and give light to those who sit in darkness and in the shadow of death, to direct and guide our feet in a straight line into the way of peace.
>
> —LUKE 1:78–79

I decree that Jesus is the Light of the world, and His light is flowing into my body, delivering me from the shadow of death and bringing me life! I will no longer walk in the dark but in the light of life "in the land of the living" (Ps. 27:13). His light is a life-giving force that can cause good health, vigor, energy, youth, and robust stamina to flood my body. His light is healing the deepest and most difficult issues in me right now.

> And six days after this, Jesus took with Him Peter and James and John his brother, and led them up on a high mountain by themselves. And His appearance underwent a change in their presence; and His face shone clear and bright like the sun....While he was still speaking, behold, a shining cloud [composed of light] overshadowed them.
>
> —MATTHEW 17:1–2, 5

I decree that God's light is overshadowing me right now. It's stronger than the best light therapy. Because of God's light my appearance is being changed. The skin on my face and body are becoming clear and bright! His light is the true source of energy that is fueling the repair and rejuvenation of damaged cells in my skin. That same light is also stimulating the production of collagen and elastin as well as boosting circulation and accelerating tissue repair. Any existing skin issue is being healed now, as the power of the light of Christ flows freely like rivers of living water from my innermost being, quickening my mortal body.

> Arise [from the depression and prostration in which circumstances have kept you—rise to a new life]! Shine (be radiant with the glory of the Lord), for your light has come, and the glory of the Lord has risen upon you!
>
> —ISAIAH 60:1

I decree that I am arising from the prostration that death and circumstances have put on me because His marvelous light is arising on me now, in Jesus' name. Amen.

Healing Commands

1. I command my soul to be healed of all sin and trauma, in Jesus' name.
2. I command all diseases, bacteria, and viruses to die, in Jesus' name.
3. I command all curses to break, in Jesus' name.
4. I command all spirits of infirmity to go, in Jesus' name.
5. I command all pain and its roots to be healed, in Jesus' name.

Now test yourself to see if your breakthrough has happened (by doing something you couldn't do before). If you have an eye issue, test to see whether your vision has improved. If you have issues with your ear(s), put your fingers in the affected ear(s) and speak this command:

I speak to the deaf and dumb spirit that is afflicting me and has disconnected me from hearing in the natural, and hearing God in the spirit realm. I command you, spirit, to come out of the place, the time, and the cause that let you in. Come out now, in Jesus' name. Now I command a creative work to happen in every part of my ear apparatus, and I command my ear(s) to open! In Jesus' name, amen. (Don't be afraid to repeat this prayer, if needed. Then test yourself!)

CHAPTER 8

LIFE-GIVING COMMUNION

COMMUNION IS A powerful blessing, as it is one of the most important and intimate ways to celebrate Christ's sacrifice. It's impossible to cover all the benefits of the Lord's Supper in this book, but let me share some key points connected to defeating the spirit of death.

The body and blood of Jesus Christ can bring life to every part of your being, including your body and soul. Jesus said of Himself, "I am the bread of life" and "I am the living bread which came down from heaven" (John 6:48, 51, NKJV). Vibrant life and, thus, power over death are contained within Christ's body and blood. Let's first look at how the blood washes, heals, and brings life to your wounded soul.

The Blood

Again, a healthy soul is a major key to defeating the spirit of death. The Bible makes clear in 3 John 2 that when your inner man prospers, your body follows suit. Sin, including generational iniquities, can wound your soul, but the blood of Jesus washes away your sins and heals you inside and out. That is why Leviticus 17:11 says, "The blood...makes atonement for the soul" (NKJV).

Jesus served His disciples during the last supper. Matthew's Gospel says that "he took the cup, and gave thanks, and gave it to them, saying, Drink ye all of it; for this is my blood of the new testament, which is shed for many for the remission of sins" (Matt. 26:27–28, KJV). The Greek word for *drink* here is *pinō*. It means "to receive into the soul what serves to refresh, strengthen, [and] nourish it."[1] As you sit in the presence of the Lord and partake of the cup of His blood, your soul is freshly

124

washed clean of the sin that wounded you so your inner man can be restored and supported in every way.

Life can be so demanding. Every day, you have multiple chances to get stressed out, offended, or even traumatized through multiple crises. Regrettably, all these things can wound your soul, then allow Satan to accuse you in court and put death on you. Therefore it's important to consistently go to the Lord's table so your soul can be *continuously* refreshed. Then you can remain healed instead of putting out fires after you've been hit with a demonic attack or a physical, mental, or emotional issue.

This is why I try to partake of His body and blood on a regular basis. Religious-minded people would disagree. However, the early church is our example: "And they steadfastly persevered, devoting themselves constantly to the instruction and fellowship of the apostles, to the breaking of bread [including the Lord's Supper] and prayers....And many wonders and signs were performed through the apostles" (Acts 2:42–43). The word translated "steadfast" is from the Greek *proskartereō*, which means to "be constantly diligent."[2] The early church was diligent to partake of Communion "constantly," and thus they walked in powerful signs, wonders, and miracles!

It's not enough to go to the table once a month or even once a week. You need to be conscientious and constant in this practice. Jesus told us why, saying, "Most assuredly, I say to you, unless you eat the flesh of the Son of Man and drink His blood, *you have no life in you*" (John 6:53, NKJV). If you don't partake of His precious sacrifice regularly, you won't appropriate the life-giving power that is in Him. If you don't want stress and trauma to continually build up in your soul and eventually cause sickness, disease, and even death, then run to His table every chance you get.

His Body Brings Life Over Death

When the first Passover was celebrated in Egypt, each part of the meal symbolized something to God's people. The bitter herbs recalled the bitterness of their slavery; the salt water represented the tears they shed during their subjugation. The main course of the meal was the lamb, the sin-bearing sacrifice that caused the judgment of God's death angel to pass over their houses.

Jesus is called "the Lamb of God who takes away the sin of the world" (John 1:29, nkjv). His body was whipped, beaten, and pierced through so that by His stripes you would be healed, and death would have to pass over your house too. When you eat the bread of Communion, you are partaking of His victory. Jesus is called the Bread of Life, so every time you eat His flesh, you receive a new inflowing of life into every bodily organ that has been touched by death.

Look at what Jesus said in John 6:

> For My flesh is true and genuine food, and My blood is true and genuine drink.... Even so whoever continues to feed on Me [whoever takes Me for his food and is nourished by Me] shall [in his turn] *live* through and because of Me.
>
> —John 6:55, 57

Jesus is claiming that whoever continues to feed on Him, meaning regularly consumes the symbols of His body and blood, will be nourished by Him and live! The word *live* (*zaō* in the Greek) means "to live...(not lifeless, not dead)."[3] As you feast at the table of the Lord, every organ in your body that was under the power of death will be restored to life! Communion will drive out the sickness and aging that death put on your tissues, blood, muscles, bones, skin, and every other part of your body and fill you with life-giving power instead.

After I had received a holy judgment against the spirit of death from the courts of heaven, I spent fifteen days taking Communion five times a day. By doing so, I was feeding on Christ, and the result was that my hot flashes finally stopped, and I began walking in a whole new level of divine health.

In 1 Corinthians 11 the apostle Paul stressed some wise instructions on how to partake of Communion. There is no way I can expound on everything he said, but I do want to look at those things that connect to judgment and the courts. For example, after Paul retold the story of the last supper in which Jesus served the bread and cup to His disciples, He gave the following admonitions:

> Therefore whoever eats this bread or drinks this cup of the Lord in an unworthy manner will be guilty of the body and blood of the Lord. But let a man examine himself, and so let him eat of the bread and drink of the cup. For he who eats and drinks in an unworthy manner eats and drinks judgment to himself, not discerning the Lord's body. For this reason many are weak and sick among you, and many sleep. For if we would judge ourselves, we would not be judged. But when we are judged, we are chastened by the Lord, that we may not be condemned with the world.
>
> —1 CORINTHIANS 11:27–32, NKJV

As a believer, you have been given the astonishing privilege of partaking in the Lord's body and blood through Communion. Therefore, you have a serious responsibility to do it with the utmost respect, awe, and reverence. Before you go to the table, you must humbly examine yourself for all sin. This includes any bitterness, offenses, and unforgiveness you are holding in your heart.

It's interesting that when Paul began his teaching on how to take Communion, he first said this:

> Now in giving these instructions I do not praise you, since you come together not for the better but for the worse. For first of all, when you come together as a church, I hear that there are divisions among you, and in part I believe it.
>
> —1 CORINTHIANS 11:17–18, NKJV

To put this in modern-day vernacular, the people in the church were throwing shade on each other. They were publicly, or even secretly among their friends, criticizing and expressing contempt for one another. They had become offended and were therefore causing strife and division.

This is one reason Paul fiercely warns us never to take the bread and the cup in an unworthy manner but to examine ourselves first. The consequence of not heeding Paul's warnings is severe. He said, "For this reason many are weak and sick among you, and many sleep" (1 Cor. 11:30, NKJV). The Greek word translated "sleep" here is *koimaō*, which means "to die"![4] This is where the church has gone wrong. We are taking the Lord's table alongside brothers or sisters with whom we are offended and even speaking ill of! Because of this we have fallen under the judgment Paul warned about: we are becoming weak and sick and are even bringing death upon ourselves!

Don't forget that Satan is a legalist who constantly goes to and fro looking for any instance of lawbreaking so he can put death on your body. Taking Communion every day is the perfect way to stop this never-ending cycle. It keeps you clean and free from the devil's accusations! However, as you come to the table, you must ask the Holy Spirit to search you for any unforgiveness, bitterness, gossip, and the like. Once you repent, you can freely partake of the living bread and destroy the power that death has over you. Just a note: You might have to ask forgiveness from the person who offended you. But wouldn't you rather do whatever it takes to please the Lord than give the devil a foothold to age and even kill you?

Don't forget that the enemy cannot judge you in court if you judge yourself first. Paul confirmed this and tied it to making self-examination part of the Lord's Supper:

> He who eats and drinks in an unworthy manner eats and drinks judgment to himself, not discerning the Lord's body. For this reason many are weak and sick among you, and many sleep. For if we would judge ourselves, we would not be judged. But when we are judged, we are chastened by the Lord, that we may not be condemned with the world.
> —1 CORINTHIANS 11:29–32, NKJV

Jesus is the living bread who came down from heaven to bring life to the world. However, you negate the life-giving benefits of Communion when you partake while holding sin, offense, or judgment in your heart.

If you first judge yourself, the devil will have no right to take you to court and have you judged. So let Communion be a sacred time of reverence, worship, and walking in the fear of the Lord. Allow Him to penetrate every area of your soul so you can discover any feelings, sins, and motives that are hidden there. You are then free to receive the inflowing of His life that gives you power over death.

Satan Uses Food to Kill

Food was the first thing Satan used to trip up the entire human race. When Adam and Eve ate from the wrong tree, we all fell. That food strategy was so effective that Satan still uses it today as one of his main weapons to control, shame, and condemn you and to bring death and unhealthy aging to your physical body.

Adam and Eve weren't the only ones tripped up by food. Isaac's son Esau was a mess! He was an angry man whose soul was controlled by food. In fact he gave up his vast inheritance for a single bowl of lentils. Regrettably, the spirit that drove Esau to forfeit his legacy is alive and well today, controlling the souls of countless people. Obesity and food-related diseases take more lives than cancer! The spirit of Esau knows this and uses it to age and kill you by enticing you to overeat, consume foods devoid of nutrition, and lust after harmful fare such as fast foods and sugary treats. This spirit also inflicts death and disease through meats full of steroids and hormones, and GMO-grown and pesticide-ridden nonorganic fruits and vegetables.

The spirit of Esau comes directly against your inheritance in Jacob, a man who was perfect, complete, and lacked nothing in physical strength and beauty. Part of Esau's assignment is to make your body the opposite of Jacob's by slowly aging you and stealing your youth, strength, and vitality. He does it through toxic food and abusive and harmful food addictions. But how does he get the right to do all that?

Esau's Soul Drove Him to Eat

The Hebrew word for *appetite* is *nephesh*, which means "soul."[5] When your soul is wounded by extreme trauma, stress, or sin, you become more vulnerable to a spirit like Esau's. It then directs your cravings, driving you to lust after unhealthy foods.

The Bible indicates that Esau's food obsession came from his soul. Genesis 25 explains why Esau so readily relinquished his firstborn blessing to his twin brother in exchange for food:

> Jacob was boiling pottage (lentil stew) one day, when Esau came from the field and was faint [with hunger]. And Esau said to Jacob, I beg of you, let me have some of that red lentil stew to eat, for I am faint and famished!...Jacob answered, Then sell me today your birthright (the rights of a firstborn). Esau said, See here, I am at the point of death; what good can this birthright do me? Jacob said, Swear to me today [that you are selling it to me]; and he swore to [Jacob] and sold him his birthright. Then Jacob gave Esau bread and stew of lentils, and he ate and drank and rose up and went his way. Thus Esau scorned his birthright as beneath his notice.
>
> —GENESIS 25:29–34

Twice this passage describes Esau as being "faint" with hunger. The Hebrew for *faint* is `ayeph, the same word used in Proverbs 25:25 to represent the thirst of a languishing soul.[6] This tells me that Esau's soul was wounded. Thus it drove him to thirst for comfort, and food became his source of relief. Sadly, he surrendered everything for it.

Communion Kicks Out Esau

When Esau forfeited his inheritance for a bowl of lentils, he claimed to be "faint and famished," or languishing. Again, this refers to the thirsty soul. However, when Jesus spoke about eating His flesh and drinking His blood, He said, "I am the bread of life. He who comes to Me shall never hunger, and he who believes in Me *shall never thirst*" (John 6:35, NKJV).

The word translated "thirst" is *dipsaō*, which refers to "those who are said to thirst, who painfully feel their want of, and eagerly long for, those things by which the soul is refreshed, supported, strengthened."[7] If, like Esau, you have soul wounds that are causing you to thirst for comfort and satisfaction, then run to the Lord's table! As you partake, your soul will be refreshed, supported, and strengthened. Then you will have nothing in common with the spirit of Esau, and it will have no legal right to drive you to eat or to put sickness on your body!

I've noticed that I tend to eat more when I am angry, stressed out, or overwhelmed. Remember what I said earlier: this is a demanding world. The everyday problems you face can wound your soul. Those wounds can then push you to eat to relieve the pressure you are feeling.

Fortunately Jesus said that anyone who comes to Him, the Bread of Life, will never hunger or thirst! Communion has power—not only to heal your soul of the ill effects of everyday life but to supernaturally curb your hunger. Don't forget what Jesus said: "My flesh is real food and my blood is real drink" (John 6:55, NIV)! When life leaves you shell-shocked and the Esau spirit entices you to overeat or consume unhealthy foods, reach for the body and blood of Jesus! It will refresh, support, and strengthen your soul, enabling you to resist the devil and even the false hunger pangs he brings.

Idols, Food, and Stolen Youth

Idolatry isn't just an Old Testament issue. Just like the ancient Israelites, who constructed statues and worshipped the demon gods they represented, we have created idols in our lives. Sadly, we sacrifice a lot of time, attention, and money to our idols, which opens us up to sin and demonic oppression.

Idols can be anything from your house and family to pharmaceuticals, fad diets, cosmetic procedures, supplements, clothing, shoes, jewelry—and the list goes on and on. These things are not bad in and of themselves, but when you become dependent on anything other than God to comfort and satisfy your soul, you could be inviting big trouble.

Why? The Bible says all idols are really demon spirits! (See

Deuteronomy 32:16–17.) When you make an idol of *anything* (even your loved ones!), you're inviting an evil spirit to attack you and bring all kinds of destruction to your life (including your finances, marriage, relationships, and businesses). The Bible proves this is true by pointing to the ancient Israelites' idolatry as the reason they were forcefully removed from their homes and taken captive in Assyria. (See 2 Kings 17:5–12.) When you submit to an idol, it can make you a prisoner in every area of your life, including your physical body.

The Bible has countless examples of diseases that demon gods can put on you. Did you know, for example, that idols are deaf, dumb, blind, and crippled? Look at these proofs:

> They did not stop worshiping demons, and idols of gold, silver, bronze, stone and wood—idols that cannot see or hear or walk.
> —REVELATION 9:20, NIV

> [Idols] have mouths, but they speak not; eyes have they, but they see not.
> —PSALM 135:16

The demon gods behind idols can cause ear and eye disorders of every kind, diseases that have a crippling effect on the body, and even speech impediments. There are many New Testament examples of people having physical illnesses due to idolatry. One is particularly startling. It's the story of "blind Bartimaeus, the son of Timaeus," who was blind from birth (Mark 10:46, NKJV). As I read this account, I couldn't help but notice that Scripture makes a point of naming the blind man's father. Intrigued, I looked up the name Timaeus and discovered that though his name means "highly prized,"[8] its prime root is the Greek word *tame'*, which means "defiled"[9]—as one is defiled by idols! I believe Timaeus worshipped idols and probably led everyone in his household to do the same. Thus his son Bartimaeus' blindness originated from an idol spirit that his family worshipped.

These spirits can bring so many more disorders upon your body! They include but are not limited to stomach problems, inflammation, skin disorders (the ancient Israelites believed leprosy was caused by the sin of idolatry), and even hemorrhoids (1 Sam. 5:9, KJV).

The simplest way to tell whether you have made something into an idol is to ask yourself some questions: Do you spend a lot of time and energy thinking about whatever it is? Are you focused on how to get it? Are you driven to find the money you need to acquire it? You might also discover that you reach for idols when you can't stand waiting any longer for God to change your situation. Consequently you go after the fast fix, which is the immediate gratification you think the idol will give you.

You will discover, however, that idols always disappoint. Unbeknown to most people, idol chasing only delays the manifestation of God's promises even more. How so? Every time you make yourself a new idol, Satan runs gleefully to court with a list of new accusations about your lawbreaking, which further delays your breakthrough.

This is a vicious cycle that every Christian has experienced. So what can you do about it?

After decades of battling my idols, I found that breaking free from their lust and control meant getting my soul healed through Communion, grace, dunamis power, and the light of Jesus Christ. Plus I had to take those demons to court repeatedly until I received a righteous verdict from heaven. (For more on this get my teachings and my soaking CD *Victory in Trials!*)

Help While You Wait

The devil relies on your falling into a never-ending pattern of idol chasing so he can continue to accuse you then put death on your body. Here's how I have gotten out of this rut: When I catch myself lusting after something, I take Communion to quench the unhealthy thirst in my soul. Then I go into the grace court and petition for grace and mercy to be poured out on me while I await the court to release a righteous verdict on my behalf.

Remember what Hebrews 4:16 says:

Let us then fearlessly and confidently and boldly draw near to the throne of grace (the throne of God's unmerited favor to us sinners), that we may receive mercy [for our failures] and find grace to help in good time for every need [appropriate help and well-timed help, coming just when we need it].

As I have said before, waiting is the hardest part, especially if you are sick, suffering some major discomfort, or even dying! When my soul starts longing after something unhealthy during the wait, I go into the court and cry, "Mercy and grace, Lord!" Then out of His goodness He gives me both, and I am empowered to press through the resistance to the manifestation of my promises. The Lord knows what you are going through! He cares for you and is ready to pour out His "well-timed help" exactly when you need it, even during your weaknesses and failures. His mercy will provide you supernatural relief from your suffering, and His grace will bestow the power and ability you need to wait in peace.

Testimony

I recently had an extraordinary victory over idol spirits by taking them to court. As a result of winning a case, I saw an awe-inspiring miracle. I was in Minnesota doing a healing session. While praying for a young man, I heard the words "numbness in the toes." I asked the man if he was experiencing such numbness, but he was not. Then a woman named Sharie, who was sitting next to us, said that she did. When I asked her for details, she told me a horrible story.

Sharie had recently had knee-replacement surgery. She said that in completing the procedure, doctors misaligned her leg bone when they sewed her up. As a result the tendons in her foot loosened when she walked, causing the bone to slip forward and protrude through her arch! You could actually see a bulge where the bone was jutting through. Because of this she could put no weight on her leg. She also had numbness and pain in her toes because the bone was pressing on a nerve and cutting off circulation in one of her arteries.

Fighting off panic, I immediately asked the Holy Spirit how to pray.

That's when I heard Him say, "She has a tree growing in the middle of her leg."

Instantly I knew what it meant. The Bible talks about the Israelites cutting down trees and carving statues out of them (Jer. 10:3; Isa. 44:14–15). Every person on the planet has some kind of idolatry in their bloodline, and it appeared that Sharie was no exception. As a result a spirit was blocking her healing. (Don't forget: the Bible says that idols cannot walk. Thus I believe the spirits behinds those idols can cause crippling disorders!)

With no time to explain, I told Sharie to repeat after me as I took her into the grace court. First, I had her repent of any idolatry in her bloodline and decree that she was under grace and not the law. Then I asked the Holy Spirit to heal her soul and take away the numbness and pain. Finally I rebuked the demonic spirit that was afflicting her; then I commanded the bone to move, and it did! (I was just as shocked as she was!) She said immediately all numbness and pain in her foot left, and she was able to put her weight on her foot and walk without hobbling. Suddenly she also realized that the bulge in her arch was totally gone! A woman sitting next to her had seen the protrusion before the miracle happened. She also came up on stage to testify that it was no longer there! Sharie's arch looked perfect. Her healing was so complete that she told us she was going to cancel the surgery she had scheduled to reposition the bone. (You can watch Sharie's testimony at the link in the notes.[10])

Food Idols and the Power of Communion

Again, you can make anything into an idol, and that includes food. Food sacrifices were an integral part of every idol-worshipping ceremony. People would dedicate their animals and part of their harvests to the demon gods they worshipped. Then as part of their worship, they would feast on those offerings so they could become one with the evil spirit. Even God's people did this, and it led to centuries of further idolatry and food sacrifices (Hos. 3:1; 1 Cor. 10:7).

In Acts 15:29 the apostle Paul warned against eating "what has been sacrificed to idols," and for good reason. When you run to food to comfort the pain in your soul, you are in essence partnering with demon gods. Look at the shocking proof from Paul in 1 Corinthians:

> What do I imply then? That food offered to idols is [intrinsically changed by the fact and amounts to] anything or that an idol itself is a [living] thing? No, I am suggesting that what the pagans sacrifice they offer [in effect] to demons (to evil spiritual powers) and not to God [at all]. *I do not want you to fellowship and be partners with diabolical spirits [by eating at their feasts].*
>
> —1 CORINTHIANS 10:19–20

When you let your wounded soul push you to make food into an idol and then feast at the table of those demons, you fellowship and become partners with them! This means they have the right to afflict every part of your life! Demons are accustomed to having food sacrificed to them, so when you keep running to their table, they gain more and more power over you with every bite.

However, Jesus revealed the way out of this idolatry, saying, "I am the bread of life. He who comes to Me shall never hunger, and he who believes in Me shall never thirst" (John 6:35, NKJV). Communion can heal your thirsty, wounded soul and break the power of its demonic hunger! Just a few verses before the passage in 1 Corinthians 10 where Paul warned us not to fellowship with diabolical spirits by eating at their feasts, he explained how the body and the blood can bring us into fellowship with Christ instead of idols!

> Therefore, my dearly beloved, shun (keep clear away from, avoid by flight if need be) any sort of idolatry (of loving or venerating anything more than God)....The cup of blessing [of wine at the Lord's Supper] upon which we ask [God's] blessing, does it not mean [that in drinking it] we participate in and share a fellowship (a communion) in the blood of Christ (the Messiah)? The bread which we break, does it not

mean [that in eating it] we participate in and share a fellowship (a communion) in the body of Christ?
—1 Corinthians 10:14, 16

When you drink the blood of Jesus and eat His body, you are participating in and fellowshipping with Christ Himself. This breaks the fellowship you formed with diabolical spirits by eating at their feasts!

When I discovered this truth about Communion's power to quash my food cravings and destroy the enemy's hold on my life, it was a game changer. I began to decree the verses in 1 Corinthians 10 while taking Communion several times a day. Within a week my eating habits changed, and my appetite lessened significantly. Plus I didn't hear the voices of those demons driving me to eat anymore. Since then the enemy has tried many times to regain his control over me. But when that happens, I go back to taking Communion and decreeing those power-packed verses. When I do this, he has to flee again!

Rebuilding Your Body in the Natural

Once you're free of Esau and other idol spirits, your desire for food will become healthy. God has created so many good things in the earth that can satisfy your taste buds and cause your youth to be restored. The Bible talks about this in Psalm 103, where it says that God "satisfieth thy mouth with good things; so that thy youth is renewed like the eagle's" (Ps. 103:5, KJV). The word translated "renewed" here is the Greek word *chadash*, which means "to rebuild...renew, repair."[11] This indicates that as you partake of healthy nutrition, your body is repaired, restructured, and transformed!

Part of destroying death is to partake of what brings life to your body. This includes organic fruits and vegetables, pesticide- and GMO-free healthy grains, superfoods, fresh fish, healthy oils and fats that feed the brain and body, and grass-fed, steroid-free meats. Every person is different, but as you explore what's best for you, you will give your body the nourishment it needs to rebuild and restore itself. Then your youth will be renewed like that of an eagle!

Idol-Busting Activation

Go back to chapter 5 and walk through the steps for entering the grace court. This time specifically focus on idols and food. Before you take Communion, make sure you examine yourself for any hidden sins or offenses. Also decree the verses and the prayer below from 1 Corinthians 10. Finally speak the soul-healing grace scriptures from chapter 6, followed by the commands provided below.

> Therefore, my dearly beloved, shun (keep clear away from, avoid by flight if need be) any sort of idolatry (of loving or venerating anything more than God).... The cup of blessing [of wine at the Lord's Supper] upon which we ask [God's] blessing, does it not mean [that in drinking it] we participate in and share a fellowship (a communion) in the blood of Christ (the Messiah)? The bread which we break, does it not mean [that in eating it] we participate in and share a fellowship (a communion) in the body of Christ?... What do I imply then? That food offered to idols is [intrinsically changed by the fact and amounts to] anything or that an idol itself is a [living] thing? No, I am suggesting that what the pagans sacrifice they offer [in effect] to demons (to evil spiritual powers) and not to God [at all]. I do not want you to fellowship and be partners with diabolical spirits [by eating at their feasts].
> —1 Corinthians 10:14, 16, 19–20

Lord, as I partake of the elements, I first repent for any instances in which I have fellowshipped and become partners with diabolical spirits by eating at their feasts. I repent now for every time I overate, ate too fast, consumed unhealthy foods, and abused foodstuffs in any way. I put myself under the grace and mercy of this court, and I decree that as I drink the cup, I am participating in and sharing fellowship (communion) in the blood of Christ. And as I partake of Your body, I am participating in and sharing fellowship in the body of Christ. Thus You are breaking the partnership and fellowship I had with diabolical spirits. I also decree that if I have feasted at the tables of any other idols, You will break that fellowship of my soul through Your body and blood. In Jesus' name, amen.

Healing Commands

1. I command my soul to be healed of trauma, in Jesus' name.

2. I command all curses to break, in Jesus' name.

3. I command all diseases, bacteria, and viruses to die, in Jesus' name.

4. I command all spirits of infirmity to go, in Jesus' name.

5. I command all pain and its roots to be healed, in Jesus' name.

6. I bind death's actions on my bodily organs, in Jesus' name. (List your organs and bind death off each one.)

7. I ask the Bread of Life to be released into every organ in my body and every part of my frame, from head to toe (including bones, blood, tissues, organs, etc.), in Jesus' name.

Now, to see if your breakthrough has occurred, test yourself by doing something you couldn't do before. Don't forget to share your testimony with us by emailing it to me at selfies@katiesouza.com. (Be sure to hold your phone in the landscape position.)

CHAPTER 9
CONQUERING BITTERNESS, WITCHCRAFT, AND PRIDE

B ITTERNESS IS ONE of the most pervasive and destructive emotions in the world today. Just go on Facebook, and you will see people spewing out hostility like vomit through their posts and comments. It's like a free-for-all. People are expressing uncontrolled rage and animosity everywhere they go in cyberspace, in public places, and even on the highway. Little do they realize that by letting themselves cut loose, they are literally inviting death to visit them and even take them out.

Bitterness is behind almost every negative emotion. The Bible calls it a root (Heb. 12:15). It lives in the soul, then causes death to rob your quality of life in the most insidious manner. Just look at this passage in Job:

> One dies in his full strength, being wholly at ease and quiet; his pails are full of milk [his veins are filled with nourishment], and the marrow of his bones is fresh and moist, whereas another man dies in bitterness of soul and never tastes of pleasure or good fortune.
>
> —Job 21:23–25

Notice the comparison Job made between these two men. The first had no bitterness, thus his veins, blood, and entire circulatory system were in perfect health. Even his bones and bone marrow were fresh and disease free. Because this man was not bitter, he was so healthy that to his dying day he was full of strength and vigor.

However, the second man was not so fortunate. Because of the bitterness in his soul, his body was not running at optimum levels like the first man. In fact he died miserably, never tasting the pleasure and good fortune God had planned for his life.

With the previous story as a gauge, you can see how bitterness can steal your youth and invite death to attack your bodily organs. Think about how important bone marrow is to your health. It strengthens the immune system by producing the red blood cells that "carry oxygen to tissues in the body," the platelets that "stop bleeding by helping blood clot," and white blood cells that "fight infections."[1] Our veins carry those bone marrow healing cells to every part of our body, and our blood contains the life-giving nutrients our bodies need to run at peak performance. Blood has the power to kill infection, repair the body, carry nutrition to the organs, muscles, and skin, and perform other vital health tasks.

However, when you allow the sin of bitterness to take hold of your soul, you are allowing death to attack the systems in your body that God created to keep you in tip-top shape. As the root of bitterness grows deeper in your soul, your vital bodily functions will break down, and you will develop rottenness of the bones, disease in the marrow, and a decrease in the life-giving power of your blood. As these body functions fail, you will age faster, and disorders of every kind will pervade your bodily organs.

It's vitally important that you be healed of all bitterness. In the rest of this chapter I am going to show you how bitterness of soul can even give evil spirits the legal right to steal your youth and put death on your body.

Witchcraft and Youthfulness

The witches who come to our meetings to sabotage us never seem to age as the years go by. I've heard many other mature, trusted ministers say the same thing. But how do these witches do it? They execute spells and perform blood sacrifices that give them supernatural power to stay young. Blood has long been considered a life-force by occult members who use it to extend their life spans and promote their own health. Witches can also put hexes and curses on other people to steal their youth, good looks, and vitality and even bring death and aging upon them. (See the curse of the "firstborn of death" in Job 18:13.)

Jezebel was the evilest queen in the Bible, and her witchcrafts were many (2 Kings 9:22). Scripture says she tore down the altar of the Lord, killed His prophets, threatened to take Elijah's life, served the god Baal through child sacrifices, and worshipped the fertility goddess Asherah, who was believed to make women's bodies fruitful and lush.

Physical beauty was of the utmost importance to Jezebel, and she used hers to manipulate and control kings, prophets, the population, and her reluctant servants. This was one of many reasons she worshipped false deities. To stay youthful looking, she used the life force within the blood of the children she sacrificed to Baal, and she relied on Asherah's demonic power to keep her body fertile, young, and fresh. Beauty was power to Jezebel. She was so reliant on her attractive features to get what she wanted that she even flaunted herself to an enemy just minutes before her death.

In the Book of 2 Kings Jehu was on his way to finally dispatch Jezebel. When she heard that he was coming, "she made herself up—put on eyeshadow and arranged her hair—and posed seductively at the window" (2 Kings 9:30, MSG). The good news is that Jehu was on a mission from God and was unaffected by her charms. Minutes later, at his command, Jezebel was thrown out that window by her own eunuchs. She was then trampled under the hooves of Jehu's horse, and her body was eaten by dogs. The point is that to her very last second, Jezebel was so confident in the power of her beauty that she even tried using it to prevent her own demise.

The ability of witches to perform spells and sacrifices to stave off death hit home for me not long ago. One night, I woke up hearing the name *Mary Worth*. I immediately remembered that as children we played a game called "Mary Worth," or "Bloody Mary." In a dark room each of us would stand in front of a mirror holding a candle. Then we would summon Mary, who was a witch. The game was meant to scare us, and it did, for sure! Some of us claimed that we actually saw Mary's face in the glass.

After I awakened that night, I immediately searched "Mary Worth" on the internet and found some eye-opening information. She was believed to be a real person, an alleged witch who kidnapped children, killed them, and drank their blood, which caused her to have power over death and remain young looking! When they finally caught her, they burned her alive at the stake. While dying, she swore that if anyone dared to say her name while looking in a mirror, she would come back and rip that person's soul to pieces.

It's alarming how many people tell me they played the Mary Worth game during childhood. The problem is that the seemingly innocent game gives the enemy a legal right to steal your youth. For me the story went even deeper. Right before this discovery I noticed that my aging process seemed to kick into high gear. Every morning when I looked in the mirror, I saw visible signs of aging on my face and body in the form of excessive sagging, lines, wrinkles, and even unusual muscle atrophy and weight gain.

Then a month or so later I ran into a woman I had known since childhood. When she walked into the room, I was totally shocked. I knew she was pushing sixty, yet she looked like she was in her early thirties! She didn't have a wrinkle on her face or neck, yet it appeared that she'd never had any cosmetic work done. Though she looked amazing, I was taken aback by a strange supernatural light emanating from her skin. It was so luminescent that even her hair glowed. When I commented on how great she looked, she said, "No one in my house ever gets old."

As our conversation continued, it was clear that she had a mixture in her, meaning that though she spoke of God, she also let slip some comments that didn't line up with the Bible or the character of Christ. (Later I went on her Facebook page and saw comments she had posted about spells, lighting candles, and healing energy.) Unfortunately she and I had a very harsh confrontation that night. She told me that I had done something years before that severely hurt her. I was taken by surprise, as I remembered having profusely praised her skills during that discussion, even offering to help her professionally. However, I had also offered some suggestions on how to improve her chances of success. At the time, I didn't realize that my advice had hurt her badly. Sadly she became extremely offended but never told me so. If she had, I would have apologized. But now no amount of repenting and asking her forgiveness was sufficient.

The night didn't end well. To be honest, I didn't handle her fierce verbal assault well either, and I finally lost my cool. Shocked at the direction the evening had taken and brokenhearted at my own reaction, I wept for an hour. Then I went to bed. Suddenly, a door opened in the spirit realm, and a dark "spirit guide" walked in. It took the form of a celebrity who has since passed on but was well known for his refusal to grow old. Immediately, I knew he was there to steal my youth and had been doing so for years without my knowledge. Startled, I immediately began decreeing the Word while commanding him to leave, in Jesus' name. He was followed by dozens of other demons, including many witchcraft spirits that came to curse me.

I don't scare easily and have dealt with countless high-level demons, but for some reason I was terrified that night. The battle continued until daybreak at five in the morning and then finally broke. That's when I remembered she and I used to play Mary Worth together as children. Apparently, over the passing years, she had let herself become extremely bitter toward me, which released curses that were stealing my youth and aging my body.

Bitterness and Witchcraft

Bitterness of any kind gives witchcraft legal ground to control or assault you. Let me explain. Acts 8:9–25 tells the story of Simon the sorcerer, who amazed people with his magic arts. Yet when he met Philip and heard the gospel, he believed and was baptized. Later, as he witnessed Peter and John laying hands on people to baptize them with the Holy Spirit, he made the mistake of offering them money to possess the same power. Peter's response was severe.

> Peter said unto him, Thy money perish with thee, because
> thou hast thought that the gift of God may be purchased with

money....Repent therefore of this thy wickedness, and pray God, if perhaps the thought of thine heart may be forgiven thee. *For I perceive that thou art in the gall of bitterness, and in the bond of iniquity.*

—Acts 8:20, 22–23, kjv

Peter essentially diagnosed what caused Simon to operate in witchcraft in the first place: he was full of bitterness. Peter went so far as to say that Simon's bitterness was an iniquity, which means that it ran in his bloodline. Bitterness is a deadly poison with deep roots. It can originate way back in your ancestry, but believe it or not, it can also come from extreme trauma. Let me explain.

When people go through a major trauma, it can not only wound their souls but also cause them to become bitter from the extraordinary pain they feel from those wounds. Regrettably, many people who practice witchcraft have extreme abuse and molestation in their histories. Because they have been grossly harmed and never received healing in their souls, they often fall into occult practices. And it's all because they became bitter through the trauma.

The reverse is just as tragic. Some people never fall into the occult, yet because they endured so much trauma and became bitter as a result, they were opened to being attacked by witchcraft. When I was just a child, I was molested by a man who was a high-level satanist. I believe that trauma and the resulting bitterness it formed in my soul enabled those spirits to steal my youth for many years.

Don't forget that the devil always needs a legal right to attack you, and he will often use painful experiences to create bitterness in your soul so he can then put a witchcraft curse on you. If you have allowed any kind of trauma to create bitterness in your heart, you need to heal those wounds, or the enemy will have legal ground to sap your strength, vigor, and beauty. Witchcraft spirits even *create* traumatic situations to get you stressed out and wounded so a bitter root can grow out of your pain.

Jezebel is one of the most powerful spirits in the world. Her attacks on God's prophets, including Elijah, were ruthless and nonstop. I wondered why I felt so terrified during the night I was ambushed. Then I remembered that Elijah, the most powerful prophet in the world, ran from Jezebel in total fear. The panic she put on him through her death threats frightened him so badly that he fled, wanting to give up and even commit suicide!

After that night, I continued to encounter occult powers that were under Jezebel's control. They would come into my room to assault me and even physically fight me. I never knew when I was going to be jumped next. This created fear in me as I battled night after night. Yet the biggest part of the warfare was to resist getting bitter about it, which of course was one of their main goals. They knew if they could make me bitter through the trauma and wound me, I would then have something in my soul in common with them, and therefore they would have dominion over me.

In the end I beat them down, and I did it by staying in God's presence through continuous worship, going to court, getting my soul healed of trauma, and keeping myself free of bitterness. After I experienced this breakthrough over witchcraft, I noticed that the rapid aging process I was experiencing ground to a halt. Then my appearance started changing. I began to look younger, and my strength and energy level increased dramatically. I believe that as you get healed of bitterness and are delivered from the attacks of witchcraft, you will experience the same thing.

Rebellion Is as the Sin of Witchcraft

I am going to talk more on bitterness later in this chapter, but first I want to touch on rebellion. The Bible says rebellion can also give witchcraft the legal right to attack you. In 1 Samuel 15 the prophet Samuel told King Saul that he was operating in witchcraft because he had not fully executed God's will in dealing with an enemy king. The repercussions were swift, with Saul losing his kingship. This is what Samuel said to Saul that day: "Rebellion is as the sin of witchcraft, and stubbornness is as idolatry and teraphim" (1 Sam. 15:23).

Remember the Bible's warning that curses cannot alight without cause

(Prov. 26:2). Rebellion at its basic level is plain lawbreaking! It wounds your soul, then gives witchcraft the power to curse you—and yes, even age you as those curses bring sickness and death on your body. During the first few years after I was released from prison, I was sick a lot. Many strange ailments came upon me for no apparent reason. That's when I learned that they were coming from a spirit of witchcraft connected to my past rebellion.

On the streets I broke every law I could. I not only used drugs but also cooked and sold them. I did collections on people who refused to pay their drug debts. I trafficked in stolen goods (including weapons) and was in and out of jail for years. My crimes escalated until the Feds busted me while I was cooking meth in a lab. The court then gave me a lengthy prison sentence. To say I was rebellious would be an understatement.

However, once I understood that I could get my soul healed of all the wounds connected to my rebellion, I had a huge breakthrough over witchcraft and the sickness it was putting on my body. From that point on I gained so much dominion over that spirit that I could break it off other people and see them healed too.

You are probably not a meth cook or a career criminal like I was. However, that doesn't mean there's no rebellion in you. Rebellion can be as simple as refusing to do something your spouse has asked you to do or driving faster than the speed limit. If you're not sure where you have been disobedient, just get in the Lord's presence and ask Him to reveal the truth so your heart can be healed.

Leviathan and Bitterness

Leviathan is another of our most formidable foes. In fact Job 41:34 (NKJV) calls him a "king," meaning he is powerful enough to bring destruction to many areas by splitting up churches, destroying businesses, ruining relationships, and causing marriages to end in divorce. Leviathan can also put death on you by causing cancer of the breast and reproductive parts and bringing about barrenness and miscarriages.

Does the Bible support these claims? Yes! Many places in Scripture speak of Leviathan, including the Book of Job. As you remember, Job experienced a lot of trauma after Satan brought accusations against him in court. As a result all his livestock were stolen, his children and servants were killed, and his physical body was attacked. Sadly, the Bible reveals that Job was wounded in his soul from those devastating traumas (Job 3:20; 7:11; 10:1; 21:5–6; 27:2)—so much so that the pain in his inner man caused him to curse the very day he was born. Let's look at what he said:

> Job opened his mouth and cursed his day (birthday). And Job said, Let the day perish wherein I was born.... Let gloom and deep darkness {the "shadow of death" in the NKJV} claim it for their own.
>
> —JOB 3:1–3, 5

Job called forth *death* upon the day he was born! In fact the entire content of Job chapter 3 is about Job cursing his birthday and wishing he had never been born. He not only cursed that day but also his mother's womb and the breasts that fed him, saying, "Let the stars of the twilight thereof be dark...because it shut not up the doors of my mother's womb....Why did the knees prevent me? Or why the breasts that I should suck?" (Job 3:9–10, 12, KJV).

Because of the soul pain his traumas caused, Job cursed his own birth and his mother's womb and breasts. He also (retroactively) called down upon himself miscarriage and early infant death:

> Let it [my birth] not come into the number of the months.
>
> —JOB 3:6, KJV

> Why died I not from the womb? Why did I not give up the ghost when I came out of the belly?
>
> —JOB 3:11, KJV

> Or as an hidden untimely birth I had not been; as infants which never saw light.
>
> —JOB 3:16, KJV

The Bible says the power of death and life are in the tongue (Prov. 18:21). That's why it's so frightening that Job would speak so carelessly. But one good thing came out of Job's rant. In his ancient wisdom he understood *which* spirit carried out the powerful curses that throughout the ages have caused women to be infertile, miscarry, or deliver babies who weren't healthy. This spirit has also caused countless men and women to suffer and even die from prostate cancer and breast, uterine, and ovarian malignancies.

In verse 8 Job revealed its name: "May those who are good at cursing curse that day. Unleash the sea beast, Leviathan, on it" (Job 3:8, MSG). Job knew Leviathan was the evil power that executed curses on men's and women's reproductive systems (including cancer of the breast, as well as ovarian, uterine, and even prostate cancer). Leviathan can cause barrenness, prevent conception, trigger miscarriages, instigate abortions, and even cause infant deaths.

Let me be clear: not all miscarriages, infertility, and cancers of the reproductive system are caused by Leviathan. If you have struggled with these issues, don't let Satan put condemnation on you and make you think it is your fault. But I have seen this spirit manifest often enough in situations where people were having reproductive issues that I felt the need to address its terrible effect in this chapter.

Like all other spirits, Leviathan can only attack you if you have something in your soul that is in common with him. And one tool it uses is bitterness. It is easy to become so traumatized from the calamities you experience in life that your soul is wounded and you become bitter.

Even Job—who despite everything he endured "did not sin with his lips" (Job 2:10)—was so devastated by his trials that he became bitter in soul and longed for death, as this portion of his lament reveals: "Wherefore is light given to him that is in misery, and life unto the bitter in soul; which long for death, but it cometh not" (Job 3:20–21, KJV). As a matter of fact Job remained bitter in soul throughout most of his story, as the following verses attest:

Therefore, I will not restrain my mouth; I will speak in the anguish of my spirit; I will complain in the bitterness of my soul.

—JOB 7:11, NKJV

My soul loathes my life; I will give free course to my complaint, I will speak in the bitterness of my soul.

—JOB 10:1, NKJV

As God lives, who has taken away my justice, and the Almighty, who has made my soul bitter.

—JOB 27:2, NKJV

Although Job grieved bitterly, he eventually came to his senses by refusing to allow the bitterness in his soul to continue and cause even more trouble in his life. (See Hebrews 12:15.) He reached out to God, proclaiming His absolute supremacy over everything and repenting for questioning God's justice and goodness (Job 42:3). When we do the opposite and allow bitterness to fester and take root in our lives, we open a door to Leviathan.

Right now countless men and women are barren or fighting cancer of some kind. Whatever their situations, I often suspect that Leviathan may be cursing them because they became bitter through the trials of life. I am not judging anyone. I know how easy it is to fall into that trap. I lost my uterus and one ovary to Leviathan because I allowed years of high-level battle and touring to make me bitter.

If you feel that the Lord is giving you revelation as you read this, you must get rid of bitterness, or Leviathan could have power to curse you. He works very closely with witchcraft spirits. That's why Job said, "May those who are good at cursing curse that day. Unleash the sea beast, Leviathan, on it" (Job 3:8, MSG).

Again, both the witchcraft and Leviathan spirits rely heavily on bitterness as their legal ground to release a curse. Bitterness can be deep in the soul, so I urge you, in addition to using the prayers at the end of this chapter, to get my teaching resource titled *Live Free: Escaping the Trap of*

Bitterness of Soul and the companion soaking CD. The soaking resource comes directly against bitterness to totally heal you and then break off every curse these spirits release in your life.

Leviathan's Pride

Leviathan not only works to kill the body through bitterness but also through sins of pride. Job 41:34 says, "He beholdeth all high things: he is a king over all the children of pride" (KJV). Leviathan gets his right to rule over your life through sins of pride, which can take many forms. Here are just a few signs that you (or someone you know) may be operating in pride:

- You must have the last word.

- You often think you are right and everyone else is wrong.

- You always want your way.

- You think of yourself before others.

- You are controlling.

- You have a religious spirit and constantly judge everyone's doctrine.

- You are self-centered and selfish.

- You like to be waited on.

- You believe that you are entitled to have whatever you want.

- You don't think you should have to help around the house, in church, at work, etc.

- You talk about yourself a lot.

- When others share about their lives, you tune out and turn your attention to other things, such as your phone.

- You speak disparagingly about your spouse, kids, family members, fellow employees, and pastors and ministers, and you speak disparagingly *to* them.

- You are arrogant and rude.

- You can't receive constructive criticism.

- You give people the silent treatment.

- You are angry and bitter, and you get offended easily.

- You hold on to unforgiveness.

These are a just a few red flags indicating that you are operating in pride and may be under the control of Leviathan. As you read through the list, you might think that you don't have any of these issues. However, it is likely that you have degrees of each one operating in your life. (Everyone does.)

The Fire of God

In dealing with and defeating Leviathan, you need not only the power of the cross but also the fire of God. Just like we've seen with dunamis, grace, and the light of Christ, God's fire is a soul-healing power.

Right before Jesus ascended into heaven, He told His disciples that He was going to send them the promise of the Holy Spirit. Then He said, "Tarry in the city of Jerusalem until you are endued with power from on high" (Luke 24:49, NKJV). The word *power* here is dunamis, which as a reminder, means "excellence of soul."[2] The promise of dunamis power descending from heaven manifested in the Upper Room when the fire of God rested on the one hundred twenty disciples who were waiting on the Lord. This means that *fire* is dunamis power.

If you could look into your spirit man where dunamis resides, you would see light, glory, and fire! That is because dunamis manifests in many ways. It is the power that executes God's grace in your life. It is also the light of Jesus and His holy fire. I believe the fire of God is dunamis power manifesting in an accelerated form. I call it "dunamis on crack."

Now let's look at what happened in the Upper Room when that dunamis fire came down on the waiting disciples:

> There appeared to them tongues resembling fire, which were separated and distributed and which settled on each one of them. And they were all filled (diffused throughout their souls) with the Holy Spirit.
>
> —ACTS 2:3–4

The fire of the Holy Spirit didn't just land on top of their heads and stay there. Rather, it diffused into their souls so they could become what dunamis means: excellent of soul. Just look at how Peter changed after that fire entered his inner man: the disciple who betrayed Jesus, hid in fear in the Upper Room, and even quit the ministry to go fishing became the man who preached to three thousand people who all got saved! And that happened only minutes after his soul was healed and made excellent by God's fire.

In Matthew 3, John the Baptist said Jesus would baptize every believer with the Holy Spirit and fire. Then John stated what the fire would do.

> I indeed baptize you with water unto repentance, but He who is coming after me is mightier than I, whose sandals I am not worthy to carry. He will baptize you with the Holy Spirit and fire. His winnowing fan is in His hand, and He will thoroughly clean out His threshing floor, and gather His wheat into the barn; but He will burn up the chaff with unquenchable fire.
>
> —MATTHEW 3:11–12, NKJV

All human beings have both chaff and wheat within them. The wheat represents the good behaviors; the chaff denotes the bad. When Jesus baptizes you with the Holy Spirit and fire, He burns up all the junk in your soul: your bad attitudes, fears, resentments, and—yes—even your pride. Fire heals your soul quickly, and because it's unquenchable, nothing can stop it. In fact fire is how you get healed of everything in your soul that you have in common with Leviathan. Isaiah 27 points to this:

> In that day [the Lord will deliver Israel from her enemies and also from the rebel powers of evil and darkness] His sharp and unrelenting, great, and strong sword will visit and punish Leviathan the swiftly fleeing serpent, Leviathan the twisting and winding serpent; and He will slay the monster that is in the sea. In that day [it will be said of the redeemed nation of Israel], a vineyard beloved and lovely; sing a responsive song to it and about it! I, the Lord, am its Keeper; I water it every moment; lest anyone harm it, I guard and keep it night and day. Wrath is not in Me. *Would that the briers and thorns [the wicked internal foe] were lined up against Me in battle! I would stride in against them; I would burn them up together.*
> —ISAIAH 27:1–4

Isaiah starts chapter 27 by telling you how God will slay Leviathan on your behalf. Then he compares God's people to a lovely vineyard that He keeps, waters, and guards day and night. Finally, in verse 4, God Himself says something very interesting about the vineyard (which we are): "Would that the briers and thorns [the wicked internal foe] were lined up against Me in battle! I would stride in against them; I would burn them up together."

Every vineyard, no matter how beautiful, has briers and thorns. Here the Lord says that we are no exception. Every believer has them. But notice here that God said those briers and thorns are "the wicked internal foe." What is that foe? The wounds in your soul! The Bible is using a metaphor of briers and thorns to describe the wickedness of your unhealed soul.

Now notice how God deals with those wounds. He burns them up with His fire! It is no coincidence that the Lord commits to torching this internal foe with His fire *right after* He promises to slay Leviathan. This confirms that the junk in your soul gives Leviathan the right to attack you. But when God's fire burns up the bitterness and pride in your inner man, you will have nothing left in common with that beast. Therefore he will have no power over you!

Don't Touch Him! Let God Do It!

Isaiah says God Himself will slay the monster from the sea with His great, sharp sword (Isa. 27:1). The Bible warns you to let God do this job because it's *His* job. You are not to rebuke, bind, or cast out Leviathan yourself. Look at these revealing verses in Job 41:

> Can you draw out the leviathan (the crocodile) with a fish-hook? Or press down his tongue with a cord?...Will he make many supplications to you [begging to be spared]? Will he speak soft words to you [to coax you to treat him kindly]? Will he make a covenant with you to take him for your servant forever? Will you play with [the crocodile] as with a bird? Or will you put him on a leash for your maidens?... *Lay your hand upon him! Remember your battle with him; you will not do [such an ill-advised thing] again!*
>
> —Job 41:1, 2–5, 8

If you have tried to cast out Leviathan, you probably remember that you got beat up pretty bad. I know I did. He is one of the few spirits that you never deal with in that manner. After all Job said that if you lay your hand on Leviathan, you will never do "such an ill-advised thing" again! Let God slay him for you. Your job in battling Leviathan is to repent of bitterness and pride and get your soul healed with the fire of God! (I encourage you to get my teaching resource *Serpent and the Soul* and the companion, *Serpent and the Soul Fire Soaker*, so you can burn away everything in your soul connected to Leviathan.)

The Power of Repentance

Bitterness can run deep in the soul. When you spend time in repentance, it will heal your soul and destroy witchcraft. Witches hate repentance! They never repent of their bitterness and rebellion, which is why they are controlled by Jezebel. The Bible says God gave Jezebel time to repent, but she refused. Prideful people don't like to repent either, which is why they are under Leviathan's control. That's why it is so important to humble yourself through repentance. Then in due time God can exalt you (1 Pet. 5:6).

This may seem contradictory to grace, but it's not. Many grace teachers tell their people they don't need to repent because they are under grace. However, Paul, who was the biggest grace teacher of all, never said that you don't need to repent. On the contrary! When he instructed the church on how to partake of Communion, he said we should *examine* ourselves, *judging* and *detecting* our shortcomings, so that we won't be judged.

Also don't forget what Matthew's Gospel says about repentance and grace: "Blessed [forgiven, refreshed by God's grace] are those who mourn [over their sins and repent], for they will be comforted [when the burden of sin is lifted]" (Matt. 5:4, AMP).

Testimony

Let me tell you a powerful testimony that will demonstrate the necessity of repenting of bitterness and having your youth restored. It happened when I was in a meeting on the East Coast. Our car pulled up to the church early, and the first thing I saw was a woman in a wheelchair waiting for the doors to open. When I went to her and asked why she was in that condition, she shared a somewhat bizarre story. Ten years earlier she had injured her foot while getting out of her car. She was immediately taken for X-rays, which revealed no broken bones. However, she was given a crutch and put on some medications to help her heal.

Unfortunately, as the months and years passed, she never got any better. In fact her other foot started hurting, even though she had not injured it. By the time I saw her, she had been in a wheelchair for three years!

As I looked at her, I heard the Holy Spirit say, "She is bitter."

I told her what I was getting, led her through a prayer of repentance, and told her to stand up. She did, for the first time in a very long time. Then we took a walk together, up and down the halls of the church. Her husband was stunned, yet she didn't seem very happy about walking. She kept looking at me saying, "It still hurts."

When I asked her how much her pain had lessened, she said it went from a level nine to a level four, which I thought was significant. Because the meeting was starting, I could not keep praying for her. But I told her very plainly *not* to get back in her wheelchair, and I promised that I would pray for her again later.

The next night, while I was speaking, I asked whether the woman and her husband were there. I was very happy to see her walk up to the stage without a wheelchair. In front of the whole room I asked her how she was feeling. She said it still hurt. Somewhat disappointed by her lack of enthusiasm about being able to walk at all, I stepped back so I could hear the Holy Spirit speak. Quickly He said, "The bitter root is still there."

Not wanting to embarrass her, I leaned in and whispered in her ear, "The Lord is saying that you are still bitter, and we need to pull out that root."

She immediately burst into tears, confirming that it was true. I continued to whisper as I led her in another prayer to get to the bottom of the bitterness. Then I commanded that root to come out! Next we took a stroll back and forth in front of the stage. After a couple of laps, I asked her how the pain was, and she said it was gone! Her husband wept.

Activations: Overcoming Bitterness, Witchcraft, and Pride

Worship is huge in breaking free from the spirits we have just studied. It took me many months of sitting at the Lord's feet to get to all of what I've shared here. (I love to soak and worship to songs about the blood when dealing with witchcraft and to fire songs when getting healed of

Leviathan's influence.) You can worship as you are led by Jesus and the Spirit.

For this time of activation, go back to chapter 5's instruction for entering the grace court. Also decree the soul-healing grace scriptures from chapter 6. Concerning witchcraft, make sure you do all the normal commands (listed below) after you worship, including commanding the curse of the bitter water to break. As for dealing with Leviathan, however, *do not* go through the list of commands and *do not bind or rebuke* that spirit. Instead, when you are done worshipping, ask God to release His great, unrelenting, sharp sword to slay that monster of the sea for you. (Make sure that when you take Communion, you also command life to flow into your organs to replace the life that curses have stolen from you.)

Healing Commands

1. I command my soul to be healed of trauma, in Jesus' name.

2. I command all curses to break, in Jesus' name.

3. I command all diseases, bacteria, and viruses to die, in Jesus' name.

4. I command all spirits of infirmity to go, in Jesus' name.

5. I command all pain and its roots to be healed, in Jesus' name.

6. I bind death's actions on my bodily organs, in Jesus' name. (List your organs and bind death off each one.)

7. I command the curse of the bitter water to be broken off my life and body by the power of Jesus's name!

8. I ask the Spirit of life to be released into every organ in my body and every part of my frame, from head to toe (including bones, blood, tissues, organs, etc.), in Jesus' name.

Now, to see if your breakthrough has occurred, test yourself by doing something you couldn't do before. Don't forget to share your testimony with us by emailing it to me at selfies@katiesouza.com. (Be sure to hold your phone in the landscape position.)

CHAPTER 10

JESUS, PROMISE MANIFESTATION, AND THE CLAIMS COURT

A SINGLE KEY UNLOCKS every door to restored youth, and His name is Jesus! Every revelation in this study has Him as its foundation because He is the only true source of vibrant and unceasing life. Here's what the Lord Himself has said about this:

> For the bread of God is he who comes down from heaven and gives life to the world.... I am the bread of life.
> —JOHN 6:33, 48, ESV

> The words that I have spoken to you are spirit and life.
> —JOHN 6:63, ESV

> I am the light of the world. Whoever follows me will not walk in darkness, but will have the light of life.
> —JOHN 8:12, ESV

> I came that they may have life and have it abundantly.
> —JOHN 10:10, ESV

> I am the resurrection and the life.
> —JOHN 11:25, ESV

> I am the way, and the truth, and the life.
> —JOHN 14:6, ESV

The Bible is replete with statements that prove Jesus is the only true source of life. One is from John's Gospel and says, "Through him all things were made; without him nothing was made that has been made. In him was life, and that life was the light of all mankind" (John 1:3–4, NIV).

Acts 3:15 says that Jesus is "the Author of life" (ESV). This means that He not only crafted the direction your earthly path would take but also wrote into your DNA (and every part of your physical being) the very essence of His life. This enables you to remain strong and healthy and is one reason Jesus is called "the last Adam...a life-giving spirit" (1 Cor. 15:45, NKJV). His Spirit, who lives in you, can quicken your mortal body with life-giving power wherever you need it (Rom. 8:11).

Jesus is *the* source of life for your body, bones, muscles, and every organ. However, there is a condition to receiving an unceasing supply of His regenerating power. Not only must you be saved, but you must *continue* to cleave to Him forever, as Jesus said:

> He who believes in Me [who cleaves to and trusts in and relies on Me] as the Scripture has said, From his innermost being shall flow [continuously] springs and rivers of living water.
>
> —JOHN 7:38

Notice that Jesus promised rivers of living water would continuously flow from your spirit into the rest of your being. However, your life experience probably does not match the truth of this verse. If it did, the ravages of aging or disease would never deplete your body. Instead you would experience His constant youth-renewing power repairing and restoring it.

So what's the catch? *Why* doesn't your experience match the promise? Jesus said it right here: those who continue to believe in, cleave to, trust in, and rely on Him will experience a nonstop flow of His life-giving power! Conversely, those who do *not* remain in the Lord will not produce such fruit. In fact they will wither and die!

I am the Vine; you are the branches. Whoever lives in Me and
I in him bears much (abundant) fruit. However, apart from
Me [cut off from vital union with Me] you can do nothing. If
a person does not dwell in Me, he is thrown out like a [broken-
off] branch, and withers; such branches are gathered up and
thrown into the fire, and they are burned.

—JOHN 15:5–6

You will only produce abundant fruit for life and health if you live
and abide in vital union with Jesus. Here's an example that's a no-brainer:
if you cut away a branch from a vine's life-giving power, the branch
dies—*period*. Jesus said unequivocally in the previous passage that such
branches wither. The Greek word for *wither* is *xērainō*, which means to
"dry up…waste away, pine away."[1] This doesn't refer to spiritual decline
only but also to physical deterioration and death. The same word is used
of the man with the withered hand, which proves that unless you stay in
vital union with Jesus, the health of your body can dry up, dangerously
decline, and waste away.

Continuing With Him Forever

I have found that after their initial salvation experience, many believers
put their need for Christ on the back burner. That's because they desire
to move into the "deeper" things of God. However, Jesus is as deep as it
gets! The mysteries contained in Him are unsearchable and indescribable
in this lifetime and even into eternity.

Sadly, I fell into this very trap. Even though my mind was built by
God to dig out the mysteries hidden in His Word, my search became
unbalanced. I forgot that Jesus said I could do *nothing* without Him.
Thus any revelation I received, no matter how astounding, would not
produce fruit, because I wasn't remaining in Him first.

Jesus confronted the Pharisees with this sobering truth. Look at it!

You search and investigate and pore over the Scriptures dili-
gently, because you suppose and trust that you have eternal

life through them. And these [very Scriptures] testify about Me! *And still you are not willing [but refuse] to come to Me, so that you might have life.*

—JOHN 5:39–40

The Pharisees probed the Scriptures deeply in an attempt to find the source of life, when all they needed to do was come to Jesus. Be assured, there is nothing wrong with searching the Word for the complex, "many-sided wisdom of God" (Eph. 3:10). Just make sure you are receiving downloads through an intimate relationship with Jesus and not sidestepping Him to get to the "good stuff." He is as good as it gets! When you make your pursuit of the Lord your number-one priority (looking for, longing for, and loving Him above all), you will find life and produce abundant fruit. And your branches (your body) will never dry up or wither.

When I returned to making Christ the center of my life, every single revelation in this book kicked in, and my health sprung up like a thirsty plant that had not been watered and fertilized enough. Of course, this growth happened because I was finally reconnected to the life-giving power of the vine.

So what does it look like to abide (or live) in Christ as John 15:5 describes? The Greek word for *abide* is *ménō*, which means "to stay...continue, dwell, endure, be present, remain...[and] tarry."[2] Those are perfect words to describe the heart position you need as you chase after Jesus. You must make His presence the place in which you *dwell*. You must choose to *endure* dry moments while you wait for Him to come. It's also vital that you *remain* in Him each and every day, long after your salvation, until you go on to glory.

If your passion for the Lord has waned since your salvation, entreat the Father right now for the grace to reignite your soul. Then you can chase after the Son like your life depends on it, *because it does.*

Worship

The Bible says that Jesus is the Son of God, the Lamb slain before the foundation of the earth, the Alpha and Omega, the First and the Last, the Messiah, King of kings, Lord of glory, Savior and Redeemer of the world, Holy One, captain of the Lord's host, and, oh, so much more (Rom. 1:4; Rev. 13:8; 22:13; John 4:25–26; Rev. 19:16; 1 Cor. 2:8; Titus 3:6; Gal. 3:13; John 6:69; Josh. 5:14). Accordingly He deserves your total praise, adoration, and worship.

Bringing a sacrifice of worship is key to abiding in the Lord. However, it requires discipline and commitment. There is a high price to pay for staying in His presence. There is also a high price for not choosing this narrow path: you will never go beyond what an ordinary human can hope for. It's in the secret place that He is made known. And trust this: He won't show up if you have cheapened your time with Him by inviting other "lovers."

Abiding means to be *present* as you worship, turning off your devices and pressing past your worries so you can focus totally on His majesty. You must never come before your Creator distracted by social media and selfish desires, treating Him like a vending machine that dispenses your list of requests. Rather, you need to worship Him, first and foremost, over every concern. When you set aside everything to give Him the exaltation He deserves, He will give you all that you desire. John 15 proves this.

> If a person does not dwell in Me, he is thrown out like a [broken-off] branch, and withers; such branches are gathered up and thrown into the fire, and they are burned. If you live in Me [abide vitally united to Me] and My words remain in you and continue to live in your hearts, ask whatever you will, and it shall be done for you.
>
> —John 15:6–7

So many people ask me why they haven't seen the manifestation of their promises yet, including restored youth. Upon examination I usually find that it is because they've left Jesus out of their spiritual pursuit. In the previous passage the Lord makes it very clear: if you do not continue to cleave to Him, your branches will be cut off. And, conversely, when you make abiding in Him your core passion, you "can ask whatever you will, and it shall be done for you"!

There is a holy order in having your prayers answered. Remaining in Jesus is first on the list, and worship is a key to abiding in Him. When you set your heart to bring a sacrifice of praise and thanksgiving to Him before all else, amazing things happen, including the renewing of your youth. Look at what materialized when a leprous man brought his worship to Jesus:

> And behold, a leper came up to Him and, *prostrating himself,*
> *worshiped Him,* saying, Lord, if You are willing, You are able
> to cleanse me by curing me. And He reached out His hand
> and touched him, saying, I am willing; be cleansed by being
> cured. And instantly his leprosy was cured and cleansed.
>
> —MATTHEW 8:2–3

Notice that the leper didn't beg Jesus to heal him. Rather, he bowed before the Lord in worship *before* he asked to be cured of his disease. When you prostrate yourself before the King of glory, recognizing His greatness, you can ask whatever you will, and it will be given to you. Worshipping Jesus releases youth-restoring power!

During my quest to defeat death, the Holy Spirit showed me that abiding in Jesus through worship and praise was crucial to my body being regenerated. One day, while worshipping Him, I saw a vision of myself crawling like a turtle to the beat of the music. When I did some research, I discovered that the leatherback turtle has a high metabolic rate and possesses a long life span, often living a hundred years!

As soon as I saw this vision, I heard the Holy Spirit tell me that if I continued to abide in Jesus' presence to the beat of worship, He would supernaturally heal my body and increase my metabolism and life span. That's when God led me to the amazing story of Caleb, who took his

inheritance in the Promised Land when he was eighty-five years old—
because he was a worshipper!

Caleb Rocks It

Caleb was forty years old when Moses sent him and eleven others to spy
out the Promised Land. Unfortunately only Caleb and Joshua believed
that God's people could take the land from the giants who lived there.
The disbelief of the majority led the nation to wander in the desert for
forty more years. Regrettably, at the end of that time, every adult but
Caleb and Joshua had died. When the next generation finally crossed
into Canaan, Caleb was as strong and healthy as he had been in his
youth! Thus he was ready to possess his inheritance in the land that
flowed with milk and honey.

> Now look at me: GOD has kept me alive, as he promised. It
> is now forty-five years since GOD spoke this word to Moses,
> years in which Israel wandered in the wilderness. And here I
> am today, eighty-five years old! I'm as strong as I was the day
> Moses sent me out. I'm as strong as ever in battle, whether
> coming or going. So give me this hill country that GOD prom-
> ised me. You yourself heard the report, that the Anakim were
> there with their great fortress cities. If GOD goes with me, I
> will drive them out, just as GOD said.
> —JOSHUA 14:10–12, MSG

Caleb was an eighty-five-year-old in a forty-year-old's body! According
to this passage, he was just as strong coming out of battle as he was going
in. In fact his body was so stout and robust that he was able to take custody of the hill country of Hebron, where the Anakim (the giants) lived!

So what was Caleb's secret? He was from the tribe of Judah. *Judah*
is *Yĕhuwdah* in the Hebrew, which means "praised"![3] Caleb was a man
of praise and worship; I believe that is why he was so young and strong
at eighty-five. Remember that Jesus is called the Lion of the tribe of
Judah. Praise brings power, authority, and youthful strength to those
who pursue the Lion in worship. Caleb's strength was beyond human.

After all he didn't defeat any ordinary enemy when claiming His inheritance. Instead he expelled three sons of Anak from the land of giants! (See Judges 1:20 and Joshua 15:14.)

Intriguingly enough, one of those giants was *Talmai*, whose name means "abounding in furrows."[4] I got a big kick out the fact that the word *furrow* means, in part, "to make wrinkles (in the face)"![5] This might seem ridiculous, but when you consistently bring a sacrifice of worship to Jesus, He defeats your enemies. Then His glory causes your physical appearance to change and become more youthful. Let me show you proof in the Word.

Worship Ushers in the Glory and Youth

The Bible makes it clear that when you bring a sacrifice of worship to Jesus, it causes God's glory to manifest:

> When the trumpeters and singers were joined in unison, making one sound to be heard in praising and thanking the Lord, and when they lifted up their voice with the trumpets and cymbals and other instruments for song and praised the Lord, saying, For He is good, for His mercy and loving-kindness endure forever, *then the house of the Lord was filled with a cloud.*
>
> —2 CHRONICLES 5:13

The glory is the presence and power of God not only in heaven but also appearing here on earth through praise and worship. When you bring a sacrifice of adoration to Jesus (whether you feel like it or not), God responds by filling your house with the greatness of His glory. The Bible says that as you dwell in the glory, you are changed into the image of Christ: "We are being transfigured into his very image as we move from one brighter level of glory to another. And this glorious transfiguration comes from the Lord, who is the Spirit" (2 Cor. 3:18, TPT).

This tells me that we are altered into His image each time we encounter the glory. This transformation isn't just spiritual but affects our entire being, including our bodies. The word for *transfigured* in the verse above is the Greek word *metamorphoō*, the same word used for how Christ's appearance changed when the glory appeared on the Mount of Transfiguration! Let's look at it.

> *His appearance underwent a change* in their presence; and *His face shone clear and bright* like the sun, and His clothing became as white as light.... While he was still speaking, behold, *a shining cloud [composed of light] overshadowed them.*
>
> —MATTHEW 17:2, 5

This passage tells me there is power in God's presence to physically transform your countenance! The account in Matthew says the glory is "composed of light." As you learned in chapter 7, the light of Christ is utilized by your skin to heal and regenerate itself. When you give Jesus your worship, His glory overshadows you with power to restore and revive your physical form.

The story of the Mount of Transfiguration as told in Luke 9 supports this thought. It reports that as Jesus was praying, "the appearance of His countenance became altered (different)" (Luke 9:29).

The Bible also says that Moses had his appearance changed in the glory:

> Moses was there with the Lord forty days and forty nights; he ate no bread and drank no water. And he wrote upon the tables the words of the covenant, the Ten Commandments. When Moses came down from Mount Sinai with the two tables of the Testimony in his hand, he did not know that the skin of his face shone and sent forth beams by reason of his speaking with the Lord.
>
> —EXODUS 34:28–29

Moses' skin shone so brightly from being in the presence of God that his face sent forth beams of light. Notice that during those forty days, Moses didn't eat. Nor did he have any water. Yet he looked amazing and was strong enough to go up and down the mountain with no problem. In the natural this would be impossible. However, in the glory it is normal to walk in supernatural strength and beauty.

The Bible promises that the glory Moses reflected is nothing compared with the glory you encounter as a partaker of the new covenant, by which you are no longer under the law.

> Now if the dispensation of death engraved in letters on stone [the ministration of the Law], was inaugurated with such glory and splendor that the Israelites were not able to look steadily at the face of Moses because of its brilliance, [a glory] that was to fade and pass away, Why should not the dispensation of the Spirit [this spiritual ministry whose task it is to cause men to obtain and be governed by the Holy Spirit] be attended with much greater and more splendid glory?
>
> —2 CORINTHIANS 3:7–8

If you missed that, read it again. When the law was originally instated, it carried so much glory that Moses' face shone with brilliance. Yet the previous verse also states that what Moses experienced does not compare to the greater glory you now have through the Holy Spirit!

Here's the bottom line: if Moses' face could be so radically changed through the ministration of the law, how much more can yours be transformed because of grace!

Fasting and the New Wineskin

Fasting is becoming increasingly popular, even in the secular world. Many are doing what's called intermittent fasting (IF) and seeing a lot of success in weight loss and weight control. Here are just a few reasons why intermittent fasting is so popular:

> According to recent studies, IF has a whole heap of benefits including inducing autophagy (the body's process of destroying unnecessary and unhealthy cells and replacing them with new, healthier cells), muscle maintenance, reduces inflammation, improves cognitive function and assists in fat loss. IF is

beneficial for retaining muscle mass, even though you're not eating frequently. It drives up the growth hormone which is a[n] anti-catabolic that helps preserves muscle mass![6]

As you can see, the benefits of intermittent fasting are substantial. It can cause the body to regenerate itself by destroying unhealthy cells and replacing them with new ones. As I undertook this practice, I saw my body steadily renew itself. I will not go into the details of how to execute IF, but the internet is loaded with advice. I suggest you consider trying it, if God gives you the grace to do so.

Fasting to See Jesus

Fasting has amazing spiritual benefits as well. First and foremost it helps you come closer to Jesus than you have ever been. But how so? As I have said before, we humans tend to use food to soothe the torment in our wounded souls. But when you pacify your pain with food instead of the Lord, you can lose your hunger to pursue Him. Physical hunger is good and, if sustained, can cause your spiritual appetite to awaken. Food creates a temporary but false sense of satisfaction. Therefore, when you go without food, you can experience the heightened, urgent sense of your need for the Lord. As a result you will be eager to chase after Him with all your heart.

As you fast from food, your cravings turn toward the One who can cause you to never hunger and thirst. Then you can experience supernatural healing in your body. Isaiah 58 says that when you fast, your light will "break forth like the morning, and your healing (your restoration and the power of a new life) shall spring forth speedily" (Isa. 58:8). Fasting will cause the power of new life to spring forth speedily in your body as old cells die off and new ones take their place. Even more importantly, it will drive you toward Jesus. Then your body will produce fruit and never wither because you are staying connected to the vine, which is Christ.

Anoint Yourself and Defeat Death

The Hebrew word for *anoint* is *mashach*, which means "to rub with oil."[7] To be anointed is to be (among other things) consecrated, set apart, and dedicated to serve God. From Scripture we know that high priests were anointed for service, as were kings (Exod. 29:7, 21, 29; 1 Sam. 16:3; 1 Kings 1:39). The ritual of anointing can be found throughout the Bible. In fact it is referenced approximately one hundred fifty times, so the topic must be important.

The term *Christ* (*Christos* in the Greek) means "anointed."[8] Jesus, who is our High Priest, was anointed during His time on earth. One powerful and poignant story involves Mary of Bethany, who poured from an alabaster jar very expensive spikenard (worth a year's wages) over the Lord's head and feet (Matt. 26:6–7; Mark 14:3; John 12:3). Jesus was deeply touched by what Mary did. The Gospel accounts report His saying that her lavish act was done in preparation for His burial, and her story would be told throughout the entire world, which it has been (Matt. 26:10–13; Mark 14:6–9).

As I read that story, I couldn't help but notice that Mary anointed Jesus after He raised her brother Lazarus from death. I think another reason Mary poured out her love on Jesus in such an extreme way is that He avenged her of the desolation that murdering spirit put on her family.

One morning, not long before I had a huge breakthrough over the spirit of death, I saw a brief vision: I was pouring a small puddle of olive oil in the palm of my hand. Then I heard the Holy Spirit say, "Anoint your whole body."

Surprisingly, this was something I had never done before, even though the Bible speaks in many places about anointing. To be honest, I never put much stock in anointing with oil to heal the sick. I'd seen thousands of miracles and had never once used oil to facilitate them. However, because God showed me that vision, I was keen to obey and find out how it was connected to having restored youth.

Anointing Heals the Sick

The anointing, which implies the smearing with oil, is often mentioned in the Bible in relation to the Holy Spirit's presence (Isa. 61:1; Acts 10:38). Thus, when you anoint yourself with oil, you are releasing the healing power of Jesus and His Spirit onto your body.

In Scripture, anointing with oil is directly connected with healing the sick. Mark 6:13 says the disciples anointed many people with oil, and they were healed of their diseases. James 5:14–15 tells sick believers to have the church elders anoint them with oil in the name of the Lord, and it guarantees that they will be made well.

In the story of Esther, oil is linked to purification, consecration, and beauty. Esther and other virgins were brought into the palace of King Xerxes so that one of them could eventually become his bride. As a part of their preparation to meet with the king, each woman received a year of beauty treatments, which consisted of being anointed with oils.

> Now when every maid's turn was come to go in to king Ahasuerus, after that she had been twelve months, according to the manner of the women, (for so were the days of their purifications accomplished, to wit, six months with oil of myrrh, and six months with sweet odours, and with other things for the purifying of the women...).
>
> —Esther 2:12, kjv

Although Esther was treated with an assortment of oils, only myrrh is mentioned by name. Why? Interestingly enough myrrh was commonly used (especially in Egypt) in the process of embalming the dead *so that the body would remain incorrupt!* Myrrh has death-defying powers. It was one of the three gifts the wise men brought to the Christ child, which begs the question of why anyone would bring an embalming oil to a newborn baby. Augustine is quoted as saying this concerning the three gifts: "Gold, as paid to a mighty King; frankincense, as offered to God; myrrh, as to one who is to die for the sins of all."[9] The wise men prophetically brought myrrh to the baby Jesus because He would die for the sins of the world, which not only brought victory over death but also incorruption of the body for those who would receive Him.

Nicodemus finished what the wise men started when he anointed Jesus' body with a mixture of myrrh and aloes following His crucifixion (John 19:39). Later the Lord was not only resurrected to new life but His body was healed and perfectly preserved. Only the scars of His sacrifice remained to remind us of what He endured for our salvation.

Myrrh and other oils contain vast healing powers over death and decay and are effectively used for everything from inflammation, infection, and pain to nourishing the skin and treating spots and wrinkles.

The future queen, Esther, bathed in oil of myrrh for six months before being presented to the king. When you anoint yourself, it brings health and life to your physical body and prepares you to meet with your King and partake of His presence and the victory over death that He won for you. I mostly anoint myself with myrrh, frankincense (one of the other gifts the wise men took to Jesus), and rose oil (the beloved bride in Song of Songs 2:1 calls herself a rose of Sharon). Many oils have amazing benefits, so I don't limit myself to those three. I do mix them with olive oil and other moisturizers. Then I anoint myself from head to toe.

Because I have a new revelation about the importance of anointing myself, I do it every day. The very first time I did it, something big happened: some of the resistance I was encountering was removed, and I started seeing even more physical changes in my body. Also, from that point on, my body would literally vibrate whenever I worshipped the Lord. During those times, I could sense the Holy Spirit releasing rivers of living water into every place I needed it.

If you are not sure whether you should go as far as I did with the daily anointing, just consider the recommendation of King Solomon: "Always be clothed in white, and *always* anoint your head with oil" (Eccles. 9:8, NIV).

The Claims Court

The last subject I am going to touch on in this book is what I've come to call the *claims court of heaven*. One day, as I became fed up with waiting on my promises, I asked the Lord whether there was a court in heaven that forced the enemy to pony up compensation for my claims faster. To be honest, I inquired half-heartedly, thinking there was no way anything like that existed. Imagine my shock when the Holy Spirit immediately gave me this powerful passage:

> [Oh, I know, I have been rash to talk out plainly this way to God!] I will [in my thinking] stand upon my post of observation and station myself on the tower or fortress, and will watch to see what He will say within me and what answer I will make [as His mouthpiece] to the perplexities of my complaint against Him. And the Lord answered me and said, Write the vision and engrave it so plainly upon tablets that everyone who passes may [be able to] read [it easily and quickly] as he hastens by. For the vision is yet for an appointed time and it hastens to the end [fulfillment]; it will not deceive or disappoint. Though it tarry, wait [earnestly] for it, because it will surely come; it will not be behindhand on its appointed day.
> —HABAKKUK 2:1–3

Believe it or not, this is about a courtroom in heaven that can legally empower believers to receive their breakthroughs in God's perfect timing!

Let me break it down. The prophet Habakkuk was anxiously awaiting the Lord's word on when His promises would manifest. Obviously the prophet was getting impatient. He even admitted being rash as he told God how irritated he was. But the Lord didn't seem to mind! Instead He immediately assured Habakkuk that although the promise would tarry, it would surely come.

Was Habakkuk being straight-out reckless as he spoke? No! The language in the Scriptures proves that he was presenting his objections in the claims court. Let me show you a few things that prove this point.

The King James Version says that Habakkuk *set* himself upon his tower when he spoke. The word translated "set" is the Hebrew *yatsab*. Included in its meaning is the idea of "a just person before a judge."[10] This indicates to me that Habakkuk had already been to the grace court, faced the charges against Israel, and been found not guilty by God's grace. Now he was ready to receive restitution, but it had not come yet, which explains his impatience. So Habakkuk went back before the judge of all the earth to seek payment on his claim and find out what the holdup was.

The Scripture says next that God *answered* Habakkuk (v. 2). The word for *answered* is the Hebrew `anah*, which is used "of a judge giving a sentence."[11] Again, this is legal language, which proves Habakkuk was in court. However, is there proof that it was the claims court?

Let's look at God's answer in Habakkuk 2:3: "For the vision is yet for an appointed time, but at the end it shall speak, and not lie: though it tarry, wait for it; because *it will surely come*, it will not tarry" (KJV). The Hebrew word translated "it will surely come" is *bow'*, which is also seen in Isaiah 3:14, Job 22:4, and Psalm 143:2. It means "to bring before a tribunal."[12] Among other things, *tribunal* is defined as "any person or institution with authority to judge, adjudicate on, *or determine claims or disputes*."[13] Thus I believe that Habakkuk was in a claims court, which (like any earthly tribunal) has the authority to force the enemy to compensate God's people, and to do it right on time.

Keys to Manifestation in the Claims Court

What are the keys to operating in this court so you can be issued your compensation? The first key involves walking in God's perfect timing. Although I was super excited to discover there is a claims court in heaven, I wasn't comforted one bit by God's answer to Habakkuk. For one thing, it meant more waiting: "though it may tarry, wait for it" (Hab. 2:3, KJV). My process had already taken so many years (decades for some promises), which is why I had come to the claims court in the first place! I wanted to know if there was a way to speed things up.

Plus, to me, God's answer to Habakkuk was confusing: "though it tarry...it will surely come, it will not tarry." Every time I read it, I saw how contradictory it sounded. Was the promise going to tarry or not? And if there was a delay, what could be done to quicken the process?

I soon realized that waiting was a two-sided coin. Nobody likes to wait, but the Bible says that waiting can be good for you and can even produce renewed youth. Again, don't forget what James 1:4 says: "But let patience have her perfect work, that ye may be perfect and entire, wanting nothing" (KJV). I love that this verses uses the word *entire*, which means "of a body without blemish or defect"![14] Plus 2 Peter 1:5–6 states that waiting builds diligence, faith, virtue, knowledge, temperance, patience, and godliness. Verse 8 says that when those characteristics abound in you, you will "neither be barren nor unfruitful in the knowledge of our Lord Jesus Christ" (2 Pet. 1:8, KJV).

Being fruitful in Jesus is the goal, so waiting can be a very good thing. It is part of yielding the harvest of abundant life in Christ. However, too much delay can devastate your faith and rob you of life-giving power. As Proverbs 13:12 says, "Hope deferred makes the heart sick, but when the desire comes, it is a tree of life" (NKJV).

The Hebrew word for *heart* in this verse is *leb*, and one of its meanings is "soul."[15] This indicates that your inner man will be wounded, thus your body will get sick if your promise is postponed too long. That's why Proverbs 13 says that a desire fulfilled is a tree of life! Once your breakthrough comes, every part of you will be infused with joy, peace, and God's life-giving power!

There is a delicate balance between God's perfect timing and waiting too long. This is why the Lord said to wait for your promise even when it tarries, because it will surely come and will not tarry. A perfectly timed waiting period is a must in order to grow in the knowledge and fullness of Christ. However, too much delay can destroy you.

Grace Until the End

So how can you position yourself to receive your breakthrough in God's perfect timetable? *You must continue to abide in Jesus and stay in His grace*. Look again at God's answer to Habakkuk, and notice the verse that immediately follows it:

> The vision is yet for an appointed time; but at the end it will speak, and it will not lie. Though it tarries, wait for it; because it will surely come, it will not tarry. Behold the proud, his soul is not upright in him; *but the just shall live by his faith.*
>
> —HABAKKUK 2:3–4, NKJV

After God says the promise will surely come, He says, "But the just shall live by his faith." What does this mean? Romans 3:24 says that you are "justified freely by His grace through the redemption that is in Christ Jesus" (NKJV). This simple statement totally proves the point of this book: your vision will manifest in God's perfect timing *if you continue* to abide in Jesus and the power of His grace!

This includes His promises of your youth being renewed. Notice that Habakkuk says the just shall *live* by faith. The word for *live* is the Hebrew *chayah*, and it is directly connected to receiving life-giving power. It means "to revive" and to "keep…(make) alive," and to "give life," and "to nourish up, preserve…quicken, recover, repair, restore (to life)," and "be whole."[16]

When you stay close to Jesus, making Him first over everything, His grace will repair, restore, and revive your body and cause you to be made completely whole. Continuing in the Lord and in His grace are the biggest keys to operating successfully in heaven's claims court. Remember that Paul warned us never to fall away from grace. Remember too that Abraham and Sarah had their youth restored through grace. Even the stricken man in Job had his flesh made fresher than a child's and was returned to the days of his youth because God was gracious.

Staying Humble Releases More Grace

If you don't stay focused on Jesus and grace while you wait, then you will get angry and bitter toward God as time slowly ticks by. Look at

Habakkuk 2:4 again: "Behold the proud, his soul is not upright in him; but the just shall live by his faith" (NKJV).

The word translated "proud" in this verse is 'aphal, and one of its meanings is "to swell."[17] Anytime you react to delay by swelling up in your soul, you resist what God is trying to develop in your character through the waiting. The Bible calls this reaction *pride*, which causes you to lose the grace you need to receive a timely manifestation. First Peter 5:5 says, "God resists the proud, but gives grace to the humble" (NKJV). Remaining humble during the pain of the process causes more grace to be released, which then triggers your promise to arrive at the perfect moment!

Manifestation Activation

Jesus is the focus of every endeavor, including the seeking of healing, restoration, and renewed youth. His promises are manifested when we follow Him with a heart of worship, patience, and trust. Bear these truths in mind as you undertake these steps:

Commit to making Jesus first in all things, from this moment on.

Anoint yourself with oil before going in to worship the King.

Seek the Holy Spirit for direction about fasting, and execute accordingly.

Continue to read and decree the grace scriptures contained in the appendix.

Be like the persistent widow: go back into the grace court until you receive your righteous verdict. Then make your case in heaven's claims court.

APPENDIX

O N THE FOLLOWING pages you will find many powerful scriptures to meditate on and decree over yourself and others. They are arranged in categories for your convenience. Take them regularly, the way you would take medicine. When you decree God's Word over yourself, I urge you to personalize it by inserting your name or changing the pronouns to make the words apply specifically to you.

Jesus heals

Yet it was the will of the Lord to bruise Him; He has put Him to grief and made Him sick. When You and He make His life an offering for sin [and He has risen from the dead, in time to come], He shall see His [spiritual] offspring, He shall prolong His days, and the will and pleasure of the Lord shall prosper in His hand.

—ISAIAH 53:10

He himself bore our sins in his body on the tree, that we might die to sin and live to righteousness. By his wounds you have been healed.

—1 PETER 2:24, ESV

Jesus passionately cried out, took his last breath, and gave up his spirit. At that moment the veil in the Holy of Holies was torn in two from the top to the bottom. The earth shook violently, rocks were split apart, and graves were opened. Then many of the holy ones who had died were brought back to life and came out of their graves. And after Jesus' resurrection, they were plainly seen by many people walking in Jerusalem.

—MATTHEW 27:50–53, TPT

But unto you who revere and worshipfully fear My name shall the Sun of Righteousness arise with healing in His wings and His beams, and you shall go forth and gambol like calves [released] from the stall and leap for joy.

—MALACHI 4:2

But so much the more the news spread abroad concerning Him, and great crowds kept coming together to hear [Him] and to be healed by Him of their infirmities.

—LUKE 5:15

Power to heal and deliver

And if the Spirit of Him Who raised up Jesus from the dead dwells in you, [then] He Who raised up Christ Jesus from the dead will also restore to life your mortal (short-lived, perishable) bodies through His Spirit Who dwells in you.

—ROMANS 8:11

He who believes in Me [who cleaves to and trusts in and relies on Me] as the Scripture has said, from his innermost being shall flow [continuously] springs and rivers of living water.

—JOHN 7:38

He called to him his twelve disciples and gave them authority over unclean spirits, to cast them out, and to heal every disease and every affliction.

—MATTHEW 10:1, ESV

His divine power has granted to us all things that pertain to life and godliness, through the knowledge of him who called us to his own glory and excellence.

—2 PETER 1:3, ESV

For God gave us a spirit not of fear but of power and love and self-control.

—2 TIMOTHY 1:7, ESV

One of those days, as He was teaching, there were Pharisees and teachers of the Law sitting by, who had come from every village and town of Galilee and Judea and from Jerusalem. And the power of the Lord was [present] with Him to heal them.

—LUKE 5:17

All the multitude were seeking to touch Him, for healing power was all the while going forth from Him and curing them all [saving them from severe illnesses or calamities].

—LUKE 6:19

Edema

It happened that when he came to the house of a certain one of the leaders of the Pharisees on a Sabbath to eat a meal, they were watching him closely. And behold, a certain man was in front of him, suffering from edema....And he took hold of him and healed him, and sent him away.

—LUKE 14:1–2, 4, LEB

Long life

You shall walk in all the way that the LORD your God has commanded you, that you may live, and that it may go well with you, and that you may live long in the land that you shall possess.

—DEUTERONOMY 5:33, ESV

Children, obey your parents in the Lord, for this is right. "Honor your father and mother (this is the first commandment with a promise), that it may go well with you and that you may live long in the land." Fathers, do not provoke your children to anger, but bring them up in the discipline and instruction of the Lord.

—EPHESIANS 6:1–4, ESV

The fear of the LORD prolongs life, but the years of the wicked will be short.

—PROVERBS 10:27, ESV

For length of days and years of life and peace they will add to you.

—PROVERBS 3:2, ESV

For by me your days will be multiplied, and years will be added to your life.

—PROVERBS 9:11, ESV

And if you will walk in my ways, keeping my statutes and my commandments, as your father David walked, then I will lengthen your days.

—1 KINGS 3:14, ESV

He asked life of you; you gave it to him, length of days forever and ever.

—PSALM 21:4, ESV

With long life I will satisfy him, and show him My salvation.

—PSALM 91:16, NKJV

My son, do not forget my teaching, but let your heart keep my commandments, for length of days and years of life and peace they will add to you.

—PROVERBS 3:1–2, ESV

Protection and deliverance from demonic sickness and death

I shall not die, but I shall live, and recount the deeds of the LORD.

—PSALM 118:17, ESV

He who dwells in the shelter of the Most High will abide in the shadow of the Almighty. I will say to the LORD, "My refuge and my fortress, my God, in whom I trust." For he will deliver you from the snare of the fowler and from the deadly pestilence. He will cover you with his pinions, and under his wings you will find refuge; his faithfulness is a shield and buckler. You will not fear the terror of the night, nor the arrow that flies by day.

—PSALM 91:1–5, ESV

The thief comes only to steal and kill and destroy. I came that they may have life and have it abundantly.

—JOHN 10:10, ESV

Because he holds fast to me in love, I will deliver him; I will protect him, because he knows my name. When he calls to me, I will answer him; I will be with him in trouble; I will rescue him and honor him. With long life I will satisfy him and show him my salvation.

—PSALM 91:14–16, ESV

When evening came, they brought to Him many who were under the power of demons, and He drove out the spirits with a word and restored to health all who were sick.

—MATTHEW 8:16

Healing and prosperity

Behold, [in the future restored Jerusalem] I will lay upon it health and healing, and I will cure them and will reveal to them the abundance of peace (prosperity, security, stability) and truth.

—JEREMIAH 33:6

And on the banks of the river on both its sides, there shall grow all kinds of trees for food; their leaf shall not fade nor shall their fruit fail [to meet the demand]. Each tree shall bring forth new fruit every month, [these supernatural qualities being] because their waters came from out of the sanctuary. And their fruit shall be for food and their leaves for healing.

— EZEKIEL 47:12

Long life is in her right hand; in her left hand are riches and honor.

—Proverbs 3:16, esv

Supernatural blessing on your food and water

You shall serve the Lord your God, and he will bless your bread and your water, and I will take sickness away from among you. None shall miscarry or be barren in your land; I will fulfill the number of your days.

—Exodus 23:25–26, esv

Skin miracles and restored youth

His flesh shall be fresher than a child's: he shall return to the days of his youth.

—Job 33:25, kjv

Behold, a leper came to him and knelt before him, saying, "Lord, if you will, you can make me clean." And Jesus stretched out his hand and touched him, saying, "I will; be clean." And immediately his leprosy was cleansed.

—Matthew 8:2–3, esv

[He exclaimed] O my love, how beautiful you are! There is no flaw in you!

—Song of Solomon 4:7

Renewed strength, energy, and vitality

He gives power to the weak, and to those who have no might He increases strength.

—Isaiah 40:29, nkjv

I can do all things through him who strengthens me.

—Philippians 4:13, esv

Even the youths shall faint and be weary, and the young men shall utterly fall, but those who wait on the Lord shall renew their strength; they shall mount up with wings like eagles, they shall run and not be weary, they shall walk and not faint.

—ISAIAH 40:30–31, NKJV

Bone health

One dies in his full strength, being wholly at ease and quiet; his pails are full of milk [his veins are filled with nourishment], and the marrow of his bones is fresh and moist, whereas another man dies in bitterness of soul and never tastes of pleasure or good fortune.

—JOB 21:23–25

Run to GOD! Run from evil! Your body will glow with health, your very bones will vibrate with life!

—PROVERBS 3:7–8, MSG

Be not wise in your own eyes; reverently fear and worship the Lord and turn [entirely] away from evil. It shall be health to your nerves and sinews, and marrow and moistening to your bones.

—PROVERBS 3:7–8

The Lord shall guide you continually and satisfy you in drought and in dry places and make strong your bones. And you shall be like a watered garden and like a spring of water whose waters fail not.

—ISAIAH 58:11

Fertility and female issues

By faith Sarah herself received power to conceive, even when she was past the age, since she considered him faithful who had promised.

—HEBREWS 11:11, ESV

Hannah became pregnant and in due time bore a son and named him Samuel [heard of God], Because, she said, I have asked him of the Lord.

—1 SAMUEL 1:20

As Jesus went, the people pressed around him. And there was a woman who had had a discharge of blood for twelve years, and though she had spent all her living on physicians, she could not be healed by anyone. She came up behind him and touched the fringe of his garment, and immediately her discharge of blood ceased.

—LUKE 8:42–44, ESV

Paralysis, crippling conditions, blindness, deafness, and inability to speak

So the report of Him spread throughout all Syria, and they brought Him all who were sick, those afflicted with various diseases and torments, those under the power of demons, and epileptics, and paralyzed people, and He healed them.

—MATTHEW 4:24

The LORD opens the eyes of the blind. The LORD lifts up those who are bowed down; the LORD loves the righteous.

—PSALM 146:8, ESV

"Behold, your God will come with vengeance, with the recompense of God. He will come and save you." Then the eyes of the blind shall be opened, and the ears of the deaf unstopped; then shall the lame man leap like a deer, and the tongue of the mute sing for joy.

—ISAIAH 35:4–6, ESV

So He replied to them, Go and tell John what you have seen and heard: the blind receive their sight, the lame walk, the lepers are cleansed, the deaf hear, the dead are raised up, and the poor have the good news (the Gospel) preached to them.

—LUKE 7:22

A great multitude came to Him, bringing with them the lame, the maimed, the blind, the dumb, and many others, and they put them down at His feet; and He cured them.

—MATTHEW 15:30

Soul and body healing

Beloved, I pray that all may go well with you and that you may be in good health, as it goes well with your soul.

—3 JOHN 2, ESV

One dies in his full strength, being wholly at ease and quiet; his pails are full of milk [his veins are filled with nourishment], and the marrow of his bones is fresh and moist, whereas another man dies in bitterness of soul and never tastes of pleasure or good fortune.

—JOB 21:23–25

He heals all your diseases

I will put none of the diseases upon you which I brought upon the Egyptians, for I am the Lord Who heals you.

—EXODUS 15:26

...Who forgives [every one of] all your iniquities, Who heals [each one of] all your diseases.

—PSALM 103:3

He went about all Galilee, teaching in their synagogues and preaching the good news (Gospel) of the kingdom, and healing every disease and every weakness and infirmity among the people.

—MATTHEW 4:23

For He had healed so many that all who had distressing bodily diseases kept falling upon Him and pressing upon Him in order that they might touch Him.

—MARK 3:10

His Word heals

My son, attend to my words; consent and submit to my sayings. Let them not depart from your sight; keep them in the center of your heart. For they are life to those who find them, healing and health to all their flesh.

—PROVERBS 4:20–22

He sends forth His word and heals them and rescues them from the pit and destruction.

—PSALM 107:20

Sin and sickness

Behold, some men were bringing on a stretcher a man who was paralyzed, and they tried to carry him in and lay him before [Jesus]. But finding no way to bring him in because of the crowd, they went up on the roof and lowered him with his stretcher through the tiles into the midst, in front of Jesus. And when He saw [their confidence in Him, springing from] their faith, He said, Man, your sins are forgiven you! And the scribes and the Pharisees began to reason and question and argue, saying, Who is this [Man] Who speaks blasphemies? Who can forgive sins but God alone? But Jesus, knowing their thoughts and questionings, answered them, Why do you question in your hearts? Which is easier: to say, Your sins are forgiven you, or to say, Arise and walk [about]? But that you may know that the Son of Man has the [power of] authority and right on earth to forgive sins, He said to the paralyzed man, I say to you, arise, pick up your litter (stretcher), and go to your own house!

—LUKE 5:18–24

Is anyone among you suffering? Let him pray. Is anyone cheerful? Let him sing praise. Is anyone among you sick? Let him call for the elders of the church, and let them pray over him, anointing him with oil in the name of the Lord. And the prayer of faith will save the one who is sick, and the Lord will raise him up. And if he has committed sins, he will be forgiven. Therefore, confess your sins to one another and pray for one another, that you may be healed. The prayer of a righteous person has great power as it is working.

—James 5:13–16, esv

Birth defects

Now Peter and John were going up to the temple at the hour of prayer, the ninth hour. And a man lame from birth was being carried, whom they laid daily at the gate of the temple that is called the Beautiful Gate to ask alms of those entering the temple. Seeing Peter and John about to go into the temple, he asked to receive alms. And Peter directed his gaze at him, as did John, and said, "Look at us." And he fixed his attention on them, expecting to receive something from them. But Peter said, "I have no silver and gold, but what I do have I give to you. In the name of Jesus Christ of Nazareth, rise up and walk!" And he took him by the right hand and raised him up, and immediately his feet and ankles were made strong. And leaping up, he stood and began to walk, and entered the temple with them, walking and leaping and praising God.

—Acts 3:1–8, esv

NOTES

Chapter 1—The New Wineskin

1. Katie Souza, "Paralyzed Larynx healed in Denver!" YouTube, May 31, 2019, https://youtu.be/URPKFWpZDhs.
2. Blue Letter Bible, s.v. *"marpê,"* accessed July 31, 2019, https://www.blueletterbible.org/lang/lexicon/lexicon.cfm?Strongs=H4832&t=KJV.

Chapter 2—The Law and the Spirit of Death

1. Katie Souza, "Dead Bone in Shoulder Revived!" YouTube, February 28, 2019, https://www.youtube.com/watch?v=lOfboyKXcBo.
2. "Necrosis and Apoptosis," Osmosis, accessed August 7, 2019, https://www.osmosis.org/learn/Necrosis_and_apoptosis.

Chapter 3—Grace Defeats the Spirit of Death

1. Blue Letter Bible, s.v. *"sōzō,"* accessed July 31, 2019, https://www.blueletterbible.org/lang/lexicon/lexicon.cfm?Strongs=G4982&t=KJV.
2. Lexico, s.v. "slave," accessed December 18, 2019, https://lexico.com/en/definition/slave.
3. John Peter Lange et al., *A Commentary on the Holy Scriptures: Genesis* (Bellingham, WA: Logos Bible Software, 2008), 491.
4. Blue Letter Bible, s.v. *"basar,"* accessed July 31, 2019, https://www.blueletterbible.org/lang/lexicon/lexicon.cfm?Strongs=H1320&t=KJV.
5. Blue Letter Bible, s.v. *"ruwtaphash,"* accessed July 31, 2019, https://www.blueletterbible.org/lang/lexicon/lexicon.cfm?Strongs=H7375&t=KJV.

Chapter 4—Satan the Legalist

1. Blue Letter Bible, s.v. *"Satanas,"* accessed August 1, 2019, https://www.blueletterbible.org/lang/lexicon/lexicon.cfm?Strongs=G4567&t=KJV.
2. Blue Letter Bible, s.v. *"katēgoreō,"* accessed August 1, 2019, https://www.blueletterbible.org/lang/lexicon/lexicon.cfm?Strongs=G2723&t=KJV.
3. Blue Letter Bible, s.v. *"katēgoreō."*

4. Blue Letter Bible, s.v. *"shûwṭ,"* accessed August 1, 2019, https://www.blueletterbible.org/lang/lexicon/lexicon.cfm?Strongs=H7751&t=KJV.
5. Blue Letter Bible, s.v. *"'amad,"* accessed August 1, 2019, https://www.blueletterbible.org/lang/lexicon/lexicon.cfm?Strongs=H5975&t=KJV.
6. Blue Letter Bible, s.v. *"exaiteō,"* accessed August 1, 2019, https://www.blueletterbible.org/lang/lexicon/lexicon.cfm?Strongs=G1809&t=KJV.
7. Blue Letter Bible, s.v. *"exaiteō."*
8. Blue Letter Bible, s.v. *"stērizō,"* accessed August 1, 2019, https://www.blueletterbible.org/lang/lexicon/lexicon.cfm?Strongs=G4741&t=KJV.
9. Blue Letter Bible, s.v. *"histēmi,"* accessed August 1, 2019, https://www.blueletterbible.org/lang/lexicon/lexicon.cfm?strongs=G2476&t=KJV.
10. Blue Letter Bible, s.v. *"katēgoreō."*
11. Blue Letter Bible, s.v. *"antidikos,"* accessed August 1, 2019, https://www.blueletterbible.org/lang/lexicon/lexicon.cfm?Strongs=G476&t=KJV.
12. Blue Letter Bible, s.v. *"ekdikeō,"* accessed August 1, 2019, https://www.blueletterbible.org/lang/lexicon/lexicon.cfm?Strongs=G1556&t=KJV, emphasis added.
13. Katie Souza, "Spirit of Death Came Off!," YouTube, August 19, 2019, https://youtu.be/OWmGyJnxWU0.

Chapter 5—The Grace Court

1. Blue Letter Bible, s.v. *"thronos,"* accessed August 1, 2019, https://www.blueletterbible.org/lang/lexicon/lexicon.cfm?Strongs=G2362&t=KJV.
2. Blue Letter Bible, s.v. *"thronos."*
3. Blue Letter Bible, , s.v. *"mishpâṭ,"* accessed August 1, 2019, https://www.blueletterbible.org/lang/lexicon/lexicon.cfm?Strongs=H4941&t=KJV.
4. Blue Letter Bible, s.v. *"mishpâṭ."*
5. Blue Letter Bible, *"tsĕdaqah,"* accessed August 1, 2019, https://www.blueletterbible.org/lang/lexicon/lexicon.cfm?Strongs=H6666&t=KJV.
6. Blue Letter Bible, s.v. *"'own,"* accessed August 1, 2019, https://www.blueletterbible.org/lang/lexicon/lexicon.cfm?Strongs=H202&t=KJV.
7. *Cambridge Dictionary*, s.v. "virile," accessed August 1, 2019, https://dictionary.cambridge.org/us/dictionary/english/virile?q=virile.
8. Blue Letter Bible, s.v. *"mishpâṭ."*

9. Blue Letter Bible, s.v. *"holoklēros,"* accessed October 24, 2019, https://www.blueletterbible.org/lang/Lexicon/Lexicon. cfm?strongs=G3648&t=KJV.

10. The word *holoklēros* is used in only one other verse in the Bible besides James 1:4. It is translated into the words *whole* and *wholly* in 1 Thessalonians 5:23: "And the very God of peace sanctify you wholly; and I pray God your whole spirit and soul and body be preserved blameless unto the coming of our Lord Jesus Christ" (KJV).

11. Blue Letter Bible, s.v. *"holoklēros,"* accessed October 24, 2019, https://www.blueletterbible.org/lang/Lexicon/Lexicon. cfm?strongs=G3648&t=KJV.

12. "Background on NSF," Gadolinium Toxicity, accessed August 13, 2019, https://gadoliniumtoxicity.com/background/nsf/.

13. Katie Souza, "God Heals Gadolinium Toxicity From MRI Contrast," YouTube, August 22, 2018, https://www.youtube.com/watch?v=UmoXQzgb1UI.

14. Dictionary.com, s.v. "advocate," accessed August 1, 2019, https://www.dictionary.com/browse/advocate?s=t.

15. Dictionary.com, s.v. "counselor," accessed August 1, 2019, https://www.dictionary.com/browse/counselor?s=t.

CHAPTER 6—TAKING YOUR BODY AND SOUL TO COURT

1. Blue Letter Bible, s.v. *"tam,"* accessed August 2, 2019, https://www.blueletterbible.org/lang/lexicon/lexicon.cfm?Strongs=H8535&t=KJV. See also, *Brown Driver Briggs* and Song of Solomon 5:2 and 6:9.

2. "Genesis 29," *Matthew Henry Commentary on the Whole Bible*, Bible Study Tools, accessed November 11, 2019, https://www.biblestudytools.com/commentaries/matthew-henry-complete/genesis/29.html.

3. Blue Letter Bible, s.v. *"yâshab,"* accessed August 2, 2019, https://www.blueletterbible.org/lang/lexicon/lexicon.cfm?Strongs=H3427&t=KJV.

4. Blue Letter Bible, s.v. *"Ya`aqob,"* accessed August 2, 2019, https://www.blueletterbible.org/lang/lexicon/lexicon.cfm?Strongs=H3290&t=KJV.

5. Dictionary.com, s.v. "supplanter," accessed August 2, 2019, https://www.dictionary.com/browse/supplanter.

6. Blue Letter Bible, s.v. *"tam."*

7. Blue Letter Bible, s.v. *"pyretós,"* accessed August 2, 2019, https://www. blueletterbible.org/lang/lexicon/lexicon.cfm?Strongs=G4446&t=KJV.

8. "In Jewish tradition, a young man began following a Rabbi between the ages of 12 and 30." Rob J. Hyndman, "How Old Were the Disciples of Jesus When They Joined Him?" Bible Q: Bible Questions Answered, November 5, 2011, http://bibleq.net/answer/4801/comment-page-1/.

9. Blue Letter Bible, s.v. *"epitimáō,"* accessed August 2, 2019, https://www. blueletterbible.org/lang/lexicon/lexicon.cfm?Strongs=G2008&t=KJV.

10. *Merriam-Webster*, s.v. "adjudge," accessed August 2, 2019, https://www. merriam-webster.com/dictionary/adjudge.

11. Blue Letter Bible, s.v. *"shĕmoneh,"* accessed August 2, 2019, https://www.blueletterbible.org/lang/lexicon/lexicon. cfm?Strongs=H8083&t=KJV.

12. Blue Letter Bible, s.v. *"tam."*

13. Blue Letter Bible, s.v. *"sheber,"* accessed August 14, 2019, https://www. blueletterbible.org/lang/lexicon/lexicon.cfm?Strongs=H7667&t=KJV.

14. Blue Letter Bible, s.v. *"dynamis,"* accessed August 2, 2019, https://www. blueletterbible.org/lang/lexicon/lexicon.cfm?Strongs=G1411&t=KJV.

15. Blue Letter Bible, s.v. *"charis,"* accessed August 14, 2019, https://www. blueletterbible.org/lang/lexicon/lexicon.cfm?Strongs=G5485&t=KJV.

16. Blue Letter Bible, s.v. *"ochleō,"* accessed August 2, 2019, https://www. blueletterbible.org/lang/lexicon/lexicon.cfm?t=nasb&strongs=g3791.

17. All of my soaking resources are available at https://katiesouza.com/ product-category/resources/soaking/.

18. Blue Letter Bible, s.v. *"asthéneia,"* accessed August 2, 2019, https://www.blueletterbible.org/lang/lexicon/lexicon. cfm?Strongs=G769&t=NASB.

19. Blue Letter Bible, s.v. *"apolyō,"* accessed August 28, 2019, https://www. blueletterbible.org/lang/lexicon/lexicon.cfm?Strongs=G630&t=KJV.

20. Katie Souza, "Oxycodone for back pain? No more! Lacey is HEALED!" YouTube, August 21, 2019, https://www.youtube.com /watch?v=SVjx0XyhH00&list=PLEE5762A11C95EE7D&index=3.

Chapter 7—The Light Brings Life

1. Blue Letter Bible, s.v. "*nekros*," accessed August 3, 2019, https://www. blueletterbible.org/lang/lexicon/lexicon.cfm?Strongs=G3498&t=NKJV.
2. Natalie Wolchover, "How Far Can the Human Eye See?" Live Science, May 7, 2012, https://www.livescience.com/33895-human-eye.html.
3. *Merriam-Webster*, s.v. "*beam*," accessed August 3, 2019, https://www. merriam-webster.com/dictionary/beam.
4. Blue Letter Bible, s.v. "*zarach*," accessed October 24, 2019, https://www.blueletterbible.org/lang/Lexicon/Lexicon. cfm?strongs=H2224&t=KJV.
5. Blue Letter Bible, s.v. "*marpe*'," accessed November 8, 2019, https:// www.blueletterbible.org/lang/lexicon/lexicon.cfm?strongs=H4832.
6. Joyce Meyer, *Battlefield of the Mind: Winning the Battle in Your Mind: Renew Your Mind Through the Power of God's Word* (New York: Faith Words, 2017).
7. Blue Letter Bible, s.v. "*marpe*'."
8. Katie Souza, "Boy with Autism Makes Tremendous Progress Thanks to Soul-Healing," YouTube, August 20, 2018, https://youtu.be/ u4jAUoIxM-k.
9. Lexico, s.v. "life," accessed December 19, 2019, https://www.lexico. com/en/definition/life.
10. Lexico, s.v. "life."
11. George Driver, "Just a Super Useful Guide to Light Therapy Treatments: What the Red, White and Blue Actually Do," *Elle*, October 30, 2018, https://www.elle.com/uk/beauty/skin/a24429127/ light-therapy-for-skin/.
12. Driver, "Just a Super Useful Guide to Light Therapy Treatments."
13. Katie Souza, "Paul Heard a sound like doors slamming when he breathed until..." YouTube, February 28, 2019, https://youtu.be/ VgMN8FEv5Nw.
14. Blue Letter Bible, .v. "*phōnē*," accessed August 3, 2019, https://www. blueletterbible.org/lang/lexicon/lexicon.cfm?Strongs=G5456&t=NKJV.
15. Blue Letter Bible, s.v. "*phainō*," accessed August 3, 2019, https://www. blueletterbible.org/lang/lexicon/lexicon.cfm?Strongs=G5316.
16. Blue Letter Bible, s.v. "*halal*," accessed August 3, 2019, https://www. blueletterbible.org/lang/lexicon/lexicon.cfm?Strongs=H1984&t=KJV.

CHAPTER 8—LIFE-GIVING COMMUNION

1. Blue Letter Bible, s.v. *"pinō,"* accessed August 3, 2019, https://www. blueletterbible.org/lang/lexicon/lexicon.cfm?Strongs=G4095&t=KJV.
2. Blue Letter Bible, s.v. *"proskartereō,"* accessed August 3, 2019, https://www.blueletterbible.org/lang/lexicon/lexicon. cfm?Strongs=G4342&t=KJV.
3. Blue Letter Bible, s.v. *"zaō,"* accessed December 26, 2019, https://www. blueletterbible.org/lang/Lexicon/Lexicon.cfm?strongs=G2198&t=KJV.
4. Blue Letter Bible, s.v. *"koimaō,"* accessed August 3, 2019, https://www. blueletterbible.org/lang/lexicon/lexicon.cfm?Strongs=G2837&t=KJV.
5. Blue Letter Bible, s.v. *"nephesh,"* accessed August 16, 2019, https://www.blueletterbible.org/lang/lexicon/lexicon. cfm?Strongs=H5315&t=KJV.
6. Blue Letter Bible, s.v. *"'ayeph,"* accessed August 16, 2019, https://www. blueletterbible.org/lang/lexicon/lexicon.cfm?strongs=H5889&ot=NASB &t=KJV#lexSearch.
7. Blue Letter Bible, s.v. *"dipsaō,"* accessed August 3, 2019, https://www. blueletterbible.org/lang/lexicon/lexicon.cfm?Strongs=G1372&t=KJV.
8. Blue Letter Bible, s.v. *"Timaios,"* accessed November 18, 2019, https://www.blueletterbible.org/lang/Lexicon/Lexicon. cfm?strongs=G5090&t=KJV.
9. Blue Letter Bible, s.v. *"tame',"* accessed August 3, 2019, https://www. blueletterbible.org/lang/lexicon/lexicon.cfm?Strongs=H2931.
10. Katie Souza, "Sharie Had a Misaligned Bone From Knee Surgery (MN WOFL)," YouTube, July 15, 2019, https://youtu.be/KWIgMi8emzE.
11. Blue Letter Bible, s.v. *"chadash,"* accessed August 3, 2019, https://www. blueletterbible.org/lang/lexicon/lexicon.cfm?Strongs=H2318&t=KJV.

CHAPTER 9—CONQUERING BITTERNESS, WITCHCRAFT, AND PRIDE

1. "What Is Bone Marrow?" UCSF Benioff Children's Hospital, accessed August 19, 2019, https://www.ucsfbenioffchildrens.org/education/what_ is_bone_marrow/.
2. Blue Letter Bible, s.v. *"dynamis."*

CHAPTER 10—Jesus, Promise Manifestation, and the Claims Court

1. Blue Letter Bible, s.v. *"xērainō,"* accessed August 24, 2019, https://www.blueletterbible.org/lang/lexicon/lexicon. cfm?Strongs=G3583&t=KJV.

2. Blue Letter Bible, s.v. *"ménō,"* accessed August 24, 2019, https://www. blueletterbible.org/lang/lexicon/lexicon.cfm?Strongs=G3306&t=KJV.

3. Blue Letter Bible, s.v. *"Yĕhuwdah,"* accessed August 24, 2019, https://www.blueletterbible.org/lang/lexicon/lexicon. cfm?Strongs=H3063&t=KJV.

4. Blue Letter Bible, s.v. *"Talmay,"* accessed August 24, 2019, https://www. blueletterbible.org/lang/lexicon/lexicon.cfm?Strongs=H8526&t=KJV.

5. Dictionary.com, s.v. "furrow," accessed August 24, 2019, https://www. dictionary.com/browse/furrow?s=t.

6. "A Day in the Life: Intermittent Fasting," *Lauren Simpson Fitness Blog*, accessed August 24, 2019, https://www.laurensimpsonfitness.com/blog/ intermittent-fasting/.

7. Blue Letter Bible, s.v. *"mashach,"* accessed August 24, 2019, https://www.blueletterbible.org/lang/lexicon/lexicon. cfm?Strongs=H4886&t=KJV.

8. Blue Letter Bible, s.v. *"Christos,"* accessed August 24, 2019, https://www.blueletterbible.org/lang/lexicon/lexicon. cfm?Strongs=G5547&t=KJV.

9. Thomas Aquinas, *Catena Aurea: Commentary on Mathew's Gospel Book 1* (n.p.: Revelation Insight Publishing, 2016), 93.

10. Blue Letter Bible, s.v. *"yatsab,"* accessed August 24, 2019, https://www. blueletterbible.org/lang/lexicon/lexicon.cfm?Strongs=H3320&t=KJV.

11. Blue Letter Bible, s.v. *"'anah,"* accessed August 24, 2019, https://www. blueletterbible.org/lang/lexicon/lexicon.cfm?Strongs=H6030&t=KJV.

12. Blue Letter Bible, s.v. *"bow',"* accessed August 24, 2019, https://www. blueletterbible.org/lang/lexicon/lexicon.cfm?Strongs=H935&t=KJV.

13. David M. Walker, *Oxford Companion to Law* (Oxford: Oxford University Press, 1980), 1239, quoted in Wikipedia, s.v. "tribunal," accessed August 24, 2019, https://en.wikipedia.org/wiki/Tribunal.

14. Blue Letter Bible, s.v. *"holoklēros,"* accessed November 1, 2019, https://www.blueletterbible.org/lang/Lexicon/Lexicon. cfm?strongs=G3648&t=KJV.

15. Blue Letter Bible, s.v. *"leb,"* accessed September 18, 2019, https://www. blueletterbible.org/lang/lexicon/lexicon.cfm?Strongs=H3820&t=KJV.

16. Blue Letter Bible, s.v. *"chayah,"* accessed September 18, 2019, https://www.blueletterbible.org/lang/lexicon/lexicon. cfm?Strongs=H2421&t=KJV.

17. Blue Letter Bible, s.v. *"`aphal,"* accessed August 24, 2019, https://www. blueletterbible.org/lang/lexicon/lexicon.cfm?Strongs=H6075&t=KJV.

ABOUT THE AUTHOR

KATIE SOUZA DIDN'T always walk in the presence and power of God. In fact, for many years she lived a violent and drug-addicted life. Katie started experimenting with drugs as a teenager, and when her media career took off, her drug use escalated. She worked as a model and actress, but drugs caused her to lose job after job, so she turned further to crime to support herself.

Katie's life consisted of drugs, clandestine laboratories, stolen vehicles, high-speed chases, gun shoot-outs, and many arrests. When she was captured by federal marshals in February 1999, she was at the end of her rope. Charged with manufacturing, conspiracy, and gun possession, Katie was sentenced to twelve and a half years in a federal prison.

The pressures of her circumstances finally drove her into the arms of God. As Katie began her long incarceration, the Holy Spirit gave her a hunger for the Word. Soon after, she started a Bible study within her cellblock. Then one night God told Katie she would have a new release date. Eighteen months later His word came to pass, and miraculously seven years was taken off of her sentence! (Her "out" date was the exact month and day God spoke to her. This is well-documented because she had announced the details to everyone she knew for months in advance!)

While still in prison, Katie began writing her first book, *The Key to Your Expected End* (The Captivity Series), which is now in huge demand by inmates around the world. In late 2006 the Lord released a healing anointing upon Katie and her team. Since that time countless people have received miracles through her conferences and teaching resources, and she has ministered in more than four thousand prisons around the world. The Lord put a mandate on Katie to bring healing to His people through international media, and in 2013 Katie and her staff began producing a television show now called *Katie*, which can be seen around the globe on major networks and viewed on her website, www.katiesouza.com. Her live teachings and miracle services also can be seen on Facebook and YouTube.

Katie and her husband, Robert, are now living out their expected end in Arizona.